Monika Steinberg

Utilizing the web for enhanced knowledge representation

Monika Steinberg

Utilizing the web for enhanced knowledge representation

Interlinking distributed resources, users and interactive tasks

Südwestdeutscher Verlag für Hochschulschriften

Impressum / Imprint
Bibliografische Information der Deutschen Nationalbibliothek: Die Deutsche Nationalbibliothek verzeichnet diese Publikation in der Deutschen Nationalbibliografie; detaillierte bibliografische Daten sind im Internet über http://dnb.d-nb.de abrufbar.
Alle in diesem Buch genannten Marken und Produktnamen unterliegen warenzeichen-, marken- oder patentrechtlichem Schutz bzw. sind Warenzeichen oder eingetragene Warenzeichen der jeweiligen Inhaber. Die Wiedergabe von Marken, Produktnamen, Gebrauchsnamen, Handelsnamen, Warenbezeichnungen u.s.w. in diesem Werk berechtigt auch ohne besondere Kennzeichnung nicht zu der Annahme, dass solche Namen im Sinne der Warenzeichen- und Markenschutzgesetzgebung als frei zu betrachten wären und daher von jedermann benutzt werden dürften.

Bibliographic information published by the Deutsche Nationalbibliothek: The Deutsche Nationalbibliothek lists this publication in the Deutsche Nationalbibliografie; detailed bibliographic data are available in the Internet at http://dnb.d-nb.de.
Any brand names and product names mentioned in this book are subject to trademark, brand or patent protection and are trademarks or registered trademarks of their respective holders. The use of brand names, product names, common names, trade names, product descriptions etc. even without a particular marking in this works is in no way to be construed to mean that such names may be regarded as unrestricted in respect of trademark and brand protection legislation and could thus be used by anyone.

Coverbild / Cover image: www.ingimage.com

Verlag / Publisher:
Südwestdeutscher Verlag für Hochschulschriften
ist ein Imprint der / is a trademark of
AV Akademikerverlag GmbH & Co. KG
Heinrich-Böcking-Str. 6-8, 66121 Saarbrücken, Deutschland / Germany
Email: info@svh-verlag.de

Herstellung: siehe letzte Seite /
Printed at: see last page
ISBN: 978-3-8381-3482-6

Zugl. / Approved by: Hannover, Leibniz Universität Hannover, Dissertation, 2011

Copyright © 2012 AV Akademikerverlag GmbH & Co. KG
Alle Rechte vorbehalten. / All rights reserved. Saarbrücken 2012

Acknowledgements

It has been a great pleasure to work at the department of System and Computer Architecture (System- und Rechnerarchitektur, SRA) during my doctoral studies.

I would like to express my particular gratitude to Jürgen Brehm (System- und Rechnerarchitektur, SRA) for his guidance, many gainful discussions about my research, a wide degree of freedom and continual inspiration, while keeping a hold on the essentials. I would also like to thank Christian Müller-Schloer (System- und Rechnerarchitektur, SRA) for giving me the chance to work in his research group. Jürgen Brehm and Christian Müller-Schloer influenced my professional and personal development in a decisive way by extraordinary commitment and helpful advice.

I am very grateful to Hans-Günter Genenger (Architekturinformatik und Darstellung, AIDA) for the large amount of freedom he gave me to pursue my own ideas and research interests, for his support, patient understanding and encouragement over many years. Additionally, I would like to thank Hans-Günter Genenger and the Information Technology in Architecture Section for enabling this interdisciplinary cooperation.

My acknowledgement goes to Nicola Henze (Learning Lab Lower Saxony, L3S) for her support in refining structure and emphases of my dissertation as well as for the excellent advices on Semantic Web related topics. Many thanks go to all my exceptional colleagues in the System and Computer Architecture group, who helped me with professional advice, motivation and good sense of humor. In particular, I would like to thank Jörg Hähner, Martin Hoffmann, Uwe Jänen, George Brancovici, and Ghadi Mahmoudi for many valuable discussions as well as especially Monika Lorenz and Lars Maasjost for their sedulous understanding, patience and support.

I would like to acknowledge the following bachelor and master students for their outstanding and very helpful contributions to the qKAI project: Nicole Ullmann, Orhan Sarioglu, Andelko Jovancevic, Martin Liro and Jan Peter Hein.

Sincere thanks are addressed to all dear friends (including little Liu) and my beloved family, especially Ursula and Reimund Steinberg, for their unwavering support and endless encouragement since long before this PhD, even since I was born.

Abstract

The Web represents an essential medium in nearly all domains in the area of information and knowledge exchange. Answers to questions on all topics, from general knowledge to specific expert know-how, are contained, either explicitly or implicitly in expert and user-generated resources. In contrast to Web 1.0, where content is explicitly created by experts, with **Social Media** (Web 2.0) the dividing line between producers and consumers is becoming increasingly indistinguishable. Knowledge is not only generated by recognized experts anymore, but also heavily influenced by collective intelligence. This brings the **quality of the content** into question, as well as the **quality of user interaction** generated by user interoperation with distributed web content. The current evolution of Social Media is being described by the term "Web 3.0" or "Social Semantic Web," whereby standardized, machine interpretable formats, semantic meaning, intelligence and user-oriented interaction complement each other ("hybrid intelligence").

Within the scope of this thesis the service-oriented mashup[1] framework, **qKAI** (qualifying Knowledge Acquisition and Inquiry), is developed for generic reuse of knowledge-oriented, **distributed web resources** in web applications and for enhanced user interaction scenarios. The combination of **standardized web technologies** and **game design mechanics** is used as an expandable concept for interactive web applications – especially in the **Social Media** area. The challenge lies in simplifying **access** to distributed web resources to enhance their **representation** and **interconnectivity**

---

[1] A mashup is a web page or application that uses and combines data, presentation or functionality from two or more sources to create new services, Wikipedia (en), 2011.

("hyperconnectivity") and to **motivate user interoperability** with these resources.

One requirement for carrying out these processes is utilizing distributed web resources for interactive knowledge-related tasks. Throughout this thesis examples of simplified information access, user interaction and motivation, and ongoing interoperability with freely available resources ("open content") are presented. Web-based game technologies are deployed as interactive knowledge systems. Distributed web resources are widely regarded as an inherent part of higher-layered applications in information and knowledge management. Knowledge engineering concerns are combined with social interaction strategies and knowledge-oriented collaboration. Based upon semantic interlinking between **resources**, **users** and **interactive** tasks, a comprehensive concept is introduced that integrates distributed web resources into enhanced knowledge representations in an incentive way. A prototypical **social web community** and stand-alone **web applications** have been developed during qKAI to implement and illustrate this concept.

qKAI web services can be reused by other web applications to integrate the preferred functionality, e.g. in the area of social online community building. The main aspects of this concept and its prototypical implementation are deduced, examined and evaluated throughout this thesis ("proof of concept").

Keywords: Knowledge Engineering, Interactive Media Systems, Distributed Web Resources, Social Media, Game Mechanics, Web Applications, Interaction, Information Quality.

Kurzfassung

Das Web stellt in nahezu allen Bereichen ein unverzichtbares Medium für Informations- und Wissensaustausch dar. Antworten auf Fragen aller Themengebiete von Allgemeinwissen bis hin zu spezifischem Fachwissen sind implizit in experten- und Nutzer-generierten Ressourcen enthalten oder verborgen. Im Gegensatz zum Web 1.0, bei dem Inhalte ausschließlich von Experten erstellt wurden, verschwimmen die Grenzen zwischen Produzenten und Konsumenten im Web 2.0 (Social Media) immer mehr, indem jeder leicht zum Akteur im heutigen Web werden kann (Mit-Mach-Web: z.B. Weblogs, Wikis). Wissen wird nicht mehr ausschließlich von ausgewiesenen Experten generiert, sondern auch stark über kollektive Intelligenz beeinflusst. Daraus ergibt sich die Frage nach **Qualität von Inhalten** aber auch nach der **Qualität möglicher Interaktionsformen** mit diesen Inhalten. Aktuell aufkommende Entwicklungen im Internet werden unter dem Schlagwort „Web 3.0" oder „Social Semantic Web" zusammengefasst, wobei sich standardisierte, maschinenlesbare Formate, Semantik, Intelligenz und anwenderorientierte Nutzerinteraktion ergänzen („Hybride Intelligenz"). Im Rahmen dieser Dissertation wurde ein Service-orientiertes Mashup-Rahmenwerk[2] **qKAI** (qualifying Knowledge Acquisition and Inquiry) für die generische Weiternutzung von wissensorientierten, verteilten Ressourcen in Webanwendungen entwickelt, um darauf aufbauend erweiterte Interaktionsszenarien zu entwickeln. Die Kombination von **Spieldesignmechanismen** und **standardisierten Webtechnologien** wird als ein gut erweiterbarer Ansatz für innovative Webanwendungen aufgegriffen. Die

---

[2] Mashup (von engl. to mash für vermischen) bezeichnet die Erstellung neuer Medieninhalte durch die nahtlose (Re-)Kombination bereits bestehender Inhalte, Wikipedia (de), 2011.

Herausforderung besteht darin, den **Zugang** zu verteilten Ressourcen im Web zu vereinfachen, ihre **Repräsentation** und **Vernetzung** („Hyperkonnektivität") zu verbessern und innovative, **motivierende Formen der Nutzerinteroperation** mit diesen Ressourcen zu schaffen. Eine Voraussetzung für die Lösung dieser Aufgabe besteht darin, verteilte Ressourcen im Web für interaktive Wissensvermittlung aufzubereiten. In dieser Arbeit wird die Vereinfachung von Informationszugang und Nutzerinteraktion, sowie die Motivation zu anhaltender Beteiligung für die Interoperation mit frei verfügbaren, verteilten Ressourcen („Open Content") exemplarisch veranschaulicht. Webbasierte **Spielmechanismen** werden als interaktives Wissenssystem eingesetzt. Insgesamt werden verteilte Web Ressourcen als inhärenter Bestandteil von höherwertigen Anwendungen in der Informations- und Wissensvermittlung betrachtet. Belange des Wissensmanagements werden so mit wissensorientierter Zusammenarbeit verwoben. Basierend auf der semantischen Verbindung zwischen **Ressourcen**, **Nutzern** und **Interaktion** wird ein übergreifendes Konzept vorgestellt, um verteilte Ressourcen im Web auf motivierende Art und Weise in Web-basierte Wissensrepräsentationen zu integrieren. Ein prototypisches, soziales **Online-Netzwerk** und **einzelne Webanwendungen** wurden im Rahmen von qKAI entwickelt, um das erarbeitete Konzept zu implementieren und zu veranschaulichen. **qKAI Web Services** können von anderen Webanwendungen genutzt werden, um gewünschte Funktionalitäten zu integrieren. Die Hauptaspekte des Konzepts und seiner prototypischen Implementierung werden im Rahmen dieser Arbeit hergeleitet, untersucht und evaluiert („Proof of Concept").

Schlüsselwörter: Wissensmodellierung, Interaktive Mediensysteme, verteilte Webressourcen, Soziale Medien, Spielmechanismen in Webanwendungen, Interaktion, Informationsqualität.

Table of Contents

Abstract I
German Abstract III
Table of Contents V
1 Introduction 1
    1.1 Motivation and Scope of Problem 6
    1.2 Research Areas 8
    1.3 Focus of Thesis and Concept 8
    1.4 Superior Hypotheses 10
    1.5 Thesis Outline 11
    1.6 Further Published Work 12
        1.6.1 International Journals 12
        1.6.2 International Conferences 12
        1.6.3 Book Chapters and Magazines 13
2 The Web as Distributed Knowledge Base 14
    2.1 Web 3.0 and Social Media 15
        2.1.1 Online Communities and Social Networks 17
        2.1.2 Folksonomies 19
    2.2 Open Content 20
    2.3 Linked Open Data (LOD) and Semantic Web 22
    2.4 The Web Behind the Scenes – A Technical View 24
        2.4.1 The Central Principle of Resources 25
        2.4.2 RESTful Web Services 26
        2.4.3 Elements of a REST Application 30
        2.4.4 Rich Internet Applications (RIA) 33
    2.5 Summary 34
3 The Convergence of User Interaction and
Game Design on the Web 35
    3.1 Interweaving Gaming Principles with Web Applications 36

      3.1.1 Interaction Design and Gaming Mechanics 37
      3.1.2 The Competition for Attention and Feedback ... 38
  3.2 Game Design Characteristics 42
      3.2.1 Basic Game Mechanics 47
      3.2.2 Reward Types 49
      3.2.3 Preproduction 52
  3.3 Games with a Purpose: Social and
      Educational Gaming 57
      3.3.1 Educational Aspects and Suitable Domains 58
      3.3.2 Game-Based Learning and
           Knowledge Games 59
  3.4 Gamification 60
  3.5 Summary 62

4 Social Media and Related Changes in Knowledge Engineering 63

  4.1 Social Media as a Knowledge Source 63
  4.2 Knowledge Engineering 64
  4.3 Social Impact 65
  4.4 The Issue of Quality 66
      4.4.1 Assessing Quality of Information
           of Autonomous Web Resources 67
      4.4.2 Information Quality Criteria and
           Open Web Content 68
      4.4.3 Categorizing Information Quality 69
  4.5 Related Work 70
  4.6 Summary 71

5 qKAI Concept: Utilizing Distributed Web Resources for Enhanced Knowledge Representation 72

  5.1 Open Content in Interactive Knowledge Systems 73
      5.1.1 Semantic Resource Annotation: A Global
           Knowledge Base from Distributed Resources .. 74
      5.1.2 Example of qKAI Resource Annotation 76

- 5.2 Rewarding Mechanisms and User Interaction 77
    - 5.2.1 Global Interaction Rewarding (GIAR) 77
    - 5.2.2 Social Interaction Taxonomy 77
    - 5.2.3 Applied Game Mechanics 84
    - 5.2.4 GIAR Components 85
    - 5.2.5 Points, Levels and Skills 87
    - 5.2.6 Feedback 96
- 5.3 User Activity and Quality of Resources 98
    - 5.3.1 Quality of Content 100
    - 5.3.2 A Three-Level Qualifying Model 102
    - 5.3.3 Quality Assessment with the Help of User Interaction 107
    - 5.3.4 Quality of Interaction 109
    - 5.3.5 Tag Quality and Ranking in Folksonomies 110
- 5.4 Related Work 124
- 5.5 Summary 124

6 The qKAI Mashup Framework 126

- 6.1 qKAI Systems Design 128
- 6.2 Applied Patterns and Techniques 130
- 6.3 Architecture Overview for Users and Agents 130
- 6.4 Hybrid Data Layer 132
    - 6.4.1 qKAI Resource Annotator 133
    - 6.4.2 qKAI Data Access Objects (DAOs) 134
- 6.5 GIAR Configuration 136
- 6.6 Tag Ranking Application Flow 140
- 6.7 qKAI Online Community Models 144
- 6.8 qKAI REST API Examples 145
    - 6.8.1 Resource Annotation Services 146
    - 6.8.2 Interaction Logging Services 150
    - 6.8.3 Interaction Stats Services 155
- 6.9 Summary 160

7 Applications Based on the qKAI Mashup Framework 163

- 7.1 Squirl: Social Interaction Rewarding Community 163
  - 7.1.1 Squirl Web Application 164
  - 7.1.2 Squirl's Start Page 165
  - 7.1.3 MySquirl - Squirl User Page 167
  - 7.1.4 Import Latest Activities 168
  - 7.1.5 Your Activity Rewards 168
  - 7.1.6 Your Activity Stats 169
  - 7.1.7 Your Squirl Profile 170
  - 7.1.8 Real Awards 171
  - 7.1.9 Critical Appraisal 171
- 7.2 MindMob: A Knowledge Community with Open Content 172
  - 7.2.1 qMAP: A Geo-Coded Visualization of Open Content 173
  - 7.2.2 qMATCH: An Assignment Quiz with Flickr Content 174
  - 7.2.3 DBpedia Guessing Games 177
- 7.3 qRANK: Qualifying and Evaluation Game 178
  - 7.3.1 qRANK: Game Description 180
  - 7.3.2 qRANK: Architecture and Backend 180
  - 7.3.3 qRANK: Game Play 181
  - 7.3.4 qRANK: Ranking the Images 183
- 7.4 Further Use Cases 183
  - 7.4.1 Information and Guiding Systems Based on Open Content 184
  - 7.4.2 Enhanced Knowledge Discovery 184
  - 7.4.3 Online Monitoring and Social Media Ranking and Analysis 184
- 7.5 Summary 185

8 qKAI Evaluation: Proof of Concept 186

- 8.1 Open Content as a Distributed Knowledge Base in Interactive Systems 186

- 8.2 The Impact of User Activity on the Quality of Resources 186
  - 8.2.1 Experiment 1: Group Ranking 187
  - 8.2.2 Result Experiment 1 187
  - 8.2.3 Experiment 2: Game-Based Picture Ranking with qRANK 188
  - 8.2.4 Result Experiment 2 189
  - 8.2.5 Resume 190
- 8.3 The Impact of Rewarding Mechanisms on User Behavior 191
  - 8.3.1 Setting 191
  - 8.3.2 Results and Conclusion 193
  - 8.3.3 Resume 196
- 8.4 Summary 197

9 Conclusion 198
- 9.1 Contributions 200
- 9.2 Future Work and Outlook 201

10 Appendices 203
- Appendix A: List of Abbreviations 203
- Appendix B: List of Figures 205
- Appendix C: List of Tables 209
- Appendix D: List of Listings 211

Bibliography 213

1 Introduction

During the last decade, the quantity and quality of information has changed drastically. We now talk about "Information Society" instead of "Industrial Society." Today, the Web offers the biggest and fastest growing information space, which is accessible to almost everyone on demand, anytime and anywhere (24/7 paradigm). **Figure 1**

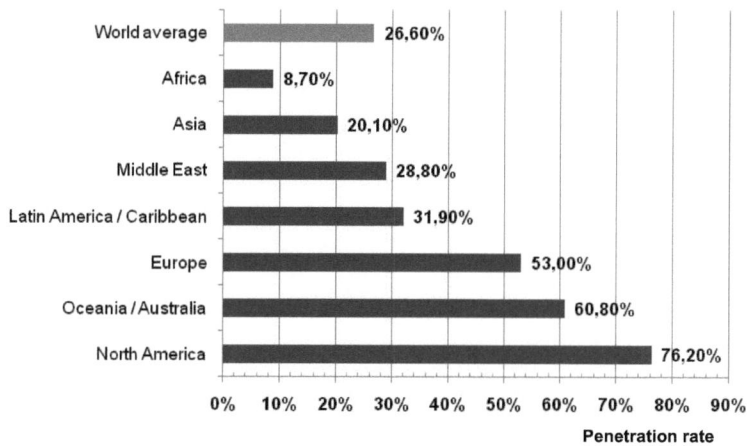

Figure 1: World Internet penetration rates by geographic regions in 2009 [1].

shows world Internet penetration rates by geographic region in 2009 [1]. According to statistics, more than 50% of Europeans use the Internet these days. In comparison, only North America and Australia showed a higher penetration rate than Europe in 2009.

In Europe, Germany ranks third after Great Britain and France regarding current Internet penetration. Germans aged 60 and older accounted for 30% of total internet penetration in 2009. The development of online usage in Germany from 1997 until 2009 is shown

1 Introduction

in percent in **Table 1** [2]. The number of internet users increased enormously in the past and will very likely continue to do so in the future. Especially remarkable is the online usage of younger people between the ages of 14 and 29, which will probably reach 100% very soon in Germany.

The indexed Web contains at least **20.57 billion web pages**. The Web can be thought of as a source of "unlimited content" that continues to grow on a daily basis in an enormous manner. The increasing interconnectivity between persons, daily life, buildings or cities with technical devices ("hyperconnectivity"), and the amount of information created by related daily interaction, grows continuously. Powerful information and communication technologies have drastically changed our society. The **Internet** has emerged as an **everyday tool** and serves as a universal network for knowledge acquisition, information exchange and working together. The line between real and virtual life is becoming increasingly blurry. Mobile devices and the growing convergence of electronic media is opening up new possibilities with the "Internet of Things," and often seem to be pervasively integrated into our daily routine.

	1997	1998	1999	2000	2001	2002	2003	2004	2005	2006	2007	2008	2009
Total	6.5	10.4	17.7	28.6	38.8	44.1	53.5	55.3	57.9	59.5	62.7	65.8	67.1
Gender													
Male	10.0	15.7	23.9	36.6	48.3	53.0	62.6	64.2	67.5	67.3	68.9	72.4	74.5
Fem.	3.3	5.6	11.7	21.3	30.1	36.0	45.2	47.3	49.1	52.4	56.9	59.6	60.1
Age													
14–19	6.3	15.6	30.0	48.5	67.4	76.9	92.1	94.7	95.7	97.3	95.8	97.2	97.5
20–29	13.0	20.7	33.0	54.6	65.5	80.3	81.9	82.8	85.3	87.3	94.3	94.8	95.2
30–39	12.4	18.9	24.5	41.1	50.3	65.6	73.1	75.9	79.9	80.6	81.9	87.9	89.4
40–49	7.7	11.1	19.6	32.2	49.3	47.8	67.4	69.9	71.0	72.0	73.8	77.3	80.2
50–59	3.0	4.4	15.1	22.1	32.2	35.4	48.8	52.7	56.5	60.0	64.2	65.7	67.4
60+	0.2	0.8	1.9	4.4	8.1	7.8	13.3	14.5	18.4	20.3	25.1	26.4	27.1

1 Introduction

Employment													
In educ.	15.1	24.7	37.9	58.5	79.4	81.1	91.6	94.5	97.4	98.6	97.6	96.7	98.0
Empl.	9.1	13.8	23.1	38.4	48.4	59.3	69.6	73.4	77.1	74.0	78.6	81.8	82.3
Pens./ unempl.	0.5	1.7	4.2	6.8	14.5	14.8	21.3	22.9	26.3	28.3	32.0	33.6	34.7

Table 1: Development in percent of online usage in Germany between 1997 and 2009 (occasional usage) [2]

To bring **global interconnectivity** and the related flood of information under control over the long term, intelligent, "smart" systems and services have been, and are continuing to be developed. These intelligent services have "proactive" knowledge available to communicate and interact with their environment. Intelligent services can make daily life, spare time, learning and working easier for users of these services.

Even access to resources or **knowledge transfer** can be simplified. Personalization of one's own information space becomes possible and new ways of managing information and knowledge can be developed with the help of **intelligent services**. Users can be assisted in the area of knowledge acquisition; the preparation and presentation of information and knowledge can be improved and conveyed, thereby creating more **incentive** and **motivation**.

The quality and relevance of web content can be enhanced by web-based, intelligent services and applications. However, there is still a strong need for further investigation and research, especially regarding new user interaction concepts and services in knowledge engineering and transfer that make use of **distributed resources as a dynamic knowledge base**.

The "Web of Content" is on its way to becoming the "Web of Applications" with on-demand infrastructure and on-demand software (Software as a Service *or* SaaS). Service-oriented offers are also appearing in the area of knowledge and learning management, but **the Web as a globally and locally connected knowledge base,**

1 Introduction

consisting of intertwined, distributed resources, has not been adequately involved so far. The content required for knowledge and learning is still created manually from scratch – often without careful attention and integration of existing and powerful web-based knowledge.

In the last few years, the principle of "hybrid intelligence" came about with the advent of **Social Media** and **Web 2.0** [3]. Hybrid interaction structures in the form of social networks combined with collective intelligence and calculable machine intelligence emerged to allow collaborative filtering and extraction of semantic meaning from our environment stemming from the overload of information. The principle of "hybrid Intelligence" allows computers and humans to do what they are best at, which means that an effective mixture of implicit and social knowledge can be realized.

Especially in the context of **Web 2.0,** we can find several examples of collectively created content ("collective intelligence"), such as wiki communities, video portals, photo collections and weblogs. **Table 2** shows occasional usage of Web 2.0 offers in Germany represented in percent. With 94%, usage of Wikipedia [4] and video portals is highest among German teenagers between the ages of 14 and 19.

	Total	Women	Men	14–19	20–29	30–39	40–49	50–59	60+
Wikipedia	65	64	67	94	77	70	62	50	39
Video portals	52	45	58	93	79	55	45	27	12
Private networks	34	36	32	81	67	29	14	12	7
Photo communities	25	25	26	42	41	20	19	19	14
Job networks	9	8	11	6	16	13	8	7	1
Weblogs	8	6	10	12	16	10	5	4	1
Bookmark collections	4	4	4	9	6	4	2	2	2

Table 2: Usage of Web 2.0 offers in percent by gender and age in Germany in 2009 (occasional usage) [2]

1 Introduction

Table 3 shows the development of frequent and occasional Web 2.0 usage in Germany between 2007 and 2009 [2]:

	Seldom to Occasional Usage			Frequent Usage (at least once a week)		
	2007	2008	2009	2007	2008	2009
Wikipedia	47	60	65	20	25	28
Video portals	34	51	52	14	21	26
Private networks	15	25	34	6	18*	24*
Photo communities	15	23	25	2	4	5
Job networks	10	6	9	4	2*	5*
Weblogs	11	6	8	3	2	3
Bookmark collections	3	3	4	0	1	2
Virtual gaming worlds	3	5	-	2	2	-

Table 3: Development of occasional and frequent usage of Web 2.0 offers in percent in Germany from 2007 to 2009 (*users with own profile) [2]

Noticeable here is the overall increasing usage for all Web 2.0 offers. It can be assumed that this trend will continue. Occasional usage of the wiki community, Wikipedia [4], is rather high with 65% in 2009. A good half of German users sometimes view video portals like YouTube [5] and even every fourth user browses web-based photo collections like Flickr [6] or Panoramio [7] now and then. Average usage of Web 2.0 offers also increased in almost every area. It is obvious that omnipresent "New Media" (compare **Chapter 4**) plays, and will continue to play a very important role in the current and future web. Furthermore, the Web influences nearly every aspect of society, such as culture, education, collaboration, communication, business, lifestyle, social habits and privacy.

The Web as a digital, computerized, interactive information and communication tool is the most powerful and pervasive example of today's "New Media". In contrast, television, traditional movies and books are not part of the definition of New Media.

1 Introduction

The German Cultural Council describes the influences of New Media as follows:

"New Media is part of daily life in our society. The Internet is used for a variety of purposes, which have now become an integral part of our culture. One example is the use of the Internet for communicating and receiving information via chat rooms, weblogs, podcasts, mobile devices, digital broadcasting and interactive computer games. Even for adults, who have mainly used the Internet and computer for work, are becoming more interested in using it for gambling, communication, and creative pursuits. Next to knowledge acquisition and self-expression, these different mediums provide opportunities for social and cultural interaction and participation."[3] [8]

1.1 Motivation and Scope of Problem

As we have seen in the introduction, the Web is omnipresent and used as a source of information and knowledge worldwide. This practice is growing continuously and is here to stay. Web 2.0 (also called Social Media) offers and online communities are being used more and more by the Digital Native generation.

Some of the questions arising from this use are:

- How can the Web as a rapidly growing and distributed knowledge base remain sustainable in higher-layered web applications?
- How can more motivation, incentive, fun and participation be brought into web-based applications and communities?

---

[3] This is the author's translation of a passage, which is taken from the "Deutscher Kulturrat" website [8].

- How can the wide range of available content be transformed into enhanced knowledge representations and distributed knowledge bases on demand?
- Which concepts and techniques are most suitable to address these challenges?

Of course, we can read a Wikipedia article sentence by sentence, or we can click through Flickr image collections, but are there methods of user interaction that are better suited to transfer the knowledge and information contained in resources?

If we found a web resource that seems to be suitable because the content matches our topic of interest, the next question we would probably ask ourselves would be about the quality and source of the content, e.g. who wrote it, how current the information is, and whether it is correct. Some of these questions might be able to be answered by automated mechanisms, e.g. metadata analysis. However, the question of whether Hannover is on the river Leine cannot be answered by a machine without further precautions.

What is the motivation for users to interact continuously with resources in communities and other applications on the Web? Maybe we can enable a user's interoperations for some higher purpose, in addition to fulfilling his request. Can we embed a user's output directly into the knowledge cycle of requested resources? User activity with a global purpose would be helpful to transfer information and to enrich content with valuable metadata in the background. Maybe users would interact more if their activities were rewarded in some global way.

Obviously, many different tasks are required to utilize arbitrarily available distributed resources for higher level, extensible and standardized applications with rich interoperation for knowledge transfer. Our research showed that there are several knowledge bases, services and software components available that are required for subtasks. Therefore, the challenge is to merge, model and expand existing services and distributed web resources to perform these tasks.

1.2 Research Areas

This thesis covers three main research areas, which are brought together in one comprehensive concept:

- Knowledge engineering (cf. **Chapter 2 and 4**)
- Distributed web resources as a knowledge base (cf. **Chapter 2**)
- Gaming mechanics in web applications as an example of enhanced user interaction (cf. **Chapter 3**)

The meaning of quality in interaction and information is dealt with in different contexts as a cross-cutting theme (cf. especially **Chapter 4.4, 5.3, 7.3**).

1.3 Focus of Thesis and Concept

This thesis is about a new concept to integrate distributed web resources as a linked knowledge base for enhanced knowledge representation. Enhanced knowledge representation here means to offer **web-based gaming** scenarios as an **interactive knowledge system** that relies on **distributed web resources**.

The challenge is to accomplish, improve and simplify access, representation and user motivation regarding interaction with autonomous, distributed web resources (instead of creating new resources from scratch).

To utilize distributed resources like Wikipedia [4] articles or multimedia from Flickr [6], semantic annotation (Linked Data [9]) is used to interlink and enrich the provenance sources by the output of user interaction and automated analysis. Game mechanics are interpreted as a subset of user interaction design (Human Computer Interaction) with enhanced user interaction quality.

1 Introduction

Gaming can be interpreted as the **supreme discipline of interaction**, because a player will play only if important aspects of the quality of the **interaction** like functionality, design, usability, incentive and fun, are fulfilled.

Review of the literature [64] [65] [74] [85] and research work showed that gaming principles are suitable for several different tasks:

- To enrich content
- To transfer knowledge
- To increase users' ongoing participation and motivation in web-based applications

Therefore, a new concept combining **knowledge engineering, distributed web resources** and **gaming mechanics** is established and examined in this thesis to take the most feasible advantage of it in every single field. Up to now, the combination of quality focused and social, game-oriented user interaction relying on distributed web resources has not been covered. In regards to knowledge transfer based on distributed web resources, the research also showed a strong need for concepts, implementations and further use case studies.

Distributed web resources are turned into gaming content to simplify information access, transfer knowledge and annotate content with the interaction output.

In this thesis, the general problem of utilizing distributed web resources for knowledge transfer is divided into three sub-problems:

- Provide standard tasks in knowledge engineering (acquisition, formalization, representation and visualization) for distributed web resources.
- Deal with incentives for user attendance while interoperating with distributed web resources (enhance the quality of interaction).

- Determine and enhance the quality of web content.

qKAI concept and mashup framework

Each of the mentioned areas is addressed in this thesis. In **Chapters 6 and 7,** the concept is illustrated and implemented with the **qKAI mashup framework** - a service-oriented software framework to handle distributed web resources in web applications with motivational user interaction.

An exemplary **online community** is developed during this thesis, demonstrating use cases and application scenarios relying on the qKAI mashup framework. Further on **qKAI** is the working title of this thesis as abbreviation of **qualifying Knowledge Acquisition and Inquiry**.

1.4 Superior Hypotheses

During the research work of this thesis, the following hypotheses emerged:

- There are many (free) resources available on the Web that should be utilized as a distributed knowledge base for further purposes, especially in the area of information and knowledge transfer.
- Without suitable and motivating user interaction and incentive, available web resources are useless or even boring for the user.
- Web-based games can be designed as interactive knowledge systems. They are suitable for improving knowledge engineering tasks, and for increasing attendance and motivation.
- The quality of interaction and information is important for the current and future web.
- Every user interaction or activity with a resource means implicit enrichment of the resource.

These hypotheses will be analyzed and examined in this thesis. Finally, they are combined into an overall concept to utilize distributed web resources for enhanced knowledge representation and higher-layered applications.

1.5 Thesis Outline

In **Chapter 1,** the motivation and scope of this thesis are introduced. In addition to the research areas involved, the overall concept of the thesis, superior hypotheses and published work is listed here.

In **Chapter 2,** the Web is presented as a distributed knowledge base. Available resources are presented, the definition of Open Content and technical aspects of today's web applications like Representational State Transfer (REST) or Linked Data principles are discussed (**Chapter 2.4**) as a foundation for further work.

In **Chapter 3,** the convergence of user interaction and gaming mechanics in web applications is discussed in detail.

In **Chapter 4,** changes in knowledge engineering by Social Media are discussed.

Chapter 5 presents the derived **qKAI concept** as a development guideline for the qKAI mashup framework – a service-oriented software framework to handle distributed web resources in web applications with motivational user interaction. The focus here is on **Open Content** as a distributed **knowledge base**, **global interaction rewarding** and the impact of user activity on the quality of information using image tag ranking in folksonomies as an example.

Chapter 6 illustrates the implemented **qKAI mashup framework** according to the concept presented in **Chapter 5**. Hybrid data management by semantic resource annotation, global interaction rewarding and the enhancement of information quality by image tag ranking and rating mechanisms are discussed in more detail, including technical aspects and examples in **Chapter 6**.

In **Chapter 7,** web **applications** and **use cases** based upon the qKAI mashup framework are introduced to illustrate how the software framework can be used while developing social web applications, e.g. the Social Interaction Rewarding Community "Squirl" is introduced along with other web applications.

Chapter 8 shows the most important **evaluation** results concerning the qKAI mashup framework and its application scenarios ("proof of concept").

Chapter 9 is the conclusion of the thesis, which includes a summary of its main points and central achievements, as well as a discussion of the work that needs to be done and future outlook.

Chapter 10 contains the following appendices: Appendix A provides a list of abbreviations; Appendix B includes figures; Appendix C contains a list of the tables found in the thesis; and Appendix D contains a list of exemplary code excerpts.

1.6 Further Published Work

1.6.1 International Journals

M. Steinberg, O. Sarioglu, J. Brehm
"Enhanced User Interaction to Qualify Web Resources by the Example of Tag Rating in Folksonomies"
In: International Journal On Advances in Intelligent Systems, vol. 3, nr. 3&4, pp. 238–257, 2010.

M. Steinberg, J. Brehm
"Utilizing Open Content for Higher-layered Rich Client Applications"
In: International Journal On Advances in Intelligent Systems, vol. 2, nr. 2&3, pp. 303–316, 2009.

1.6.2 International Conferences

M. Steinberg, N. Ullmann, J. Brehm
"A Social Interaction Taxonomy: Classifying User Interaction Tasks

in Web Applications"
In: Proc. DigitalWorld 2011, International Conference on Mobile, Hybrid, and On-line Learning, eLmL, Guadeloupe, ISBN: 978-1-61208-003-1, pp. 25–30, (Best Paper Award), 2011.

M. Steinberg, J. Brehm
"Towards Enhanced User Interaction to Qualify Web Resources for Higher-layered Applications"
In: Proc. DigitalWorld 2010, International Conference on Mobile, Hybrid, and On-line Learning, eLmL, Neth. Antilles, ISBN: 978-0-7695-3955-3, pp. 105–110, (Best Paper Award), 2010.

M. Steinberg, J. Brehm
"Social Educational Games Based on Open Content"
In: Proc. International Conference on Intelligent Networking and Collaborative Systems (INCoS), Spain, ISBN: 978-1-4244-5165-4, pp. 255–258, 2009.

M. Steinberg, J. Brehm
"Towards Utilizing Open Data for Interactive Knowledge Transfer"
In: Proc. DigitalWorld 2009, International Conference on Mobile, Hybrid, and On-line Learning (eLmL), Mexico, ISBN: 978-0-7695-3528-9, pp. 61–66, (Best Paper Award), 2009.

1.6.3 Book Chapters and Magazines

M. Steinberg, J. Brehm
"A Hybrid Data Layer to Utilize Open Content for Higher-layered Applications"
In: Data management in the Semantic Web, Nova Science Publishers, volume editors: Hai Jin, Zehua Lv, ISBN: 978-1-61122-862-5, chapter 14, 2011.

J. Brehm, M. Steinberg
"Online Communities im Kontext von Ambient Assisted Living"
In: APS+PC Nachrichten (GI), Jahrgang 19, Heft 1, ISSN 0941-9519, pp. 21-32, 2010.

2 The Web as Distributed Knowledge Base

The *World Wide Web* (*WWW* or commonly known as "The Web") is a hypermedia system consisting of interactive, non-linear media with distributed, intertwined resources. Current web content is much more than just hypertext created only by experts (like it was at the very beginning of the Web in 1991 [10]). Next to pure text elements, today's Web consists of a great deal of collectively created multimedia content like pictures, videos, animations, sounds or maps that offer a wide range of opportunities, which can be used for many purposes. We can find related and helpful content on the Web for

Figure 2: Web 3.0 tag cloud (created with Wordle [13])

practically anything, whether it be a nice hotel to spend our next holiday, the meaning of a French word, the architectural history of Berlin, or the best price for a book, the Web is a vast information space that meets our information needs. In Web 2.0 [11] we do not just find the information itself, we even find other people's opinions and experiences with it, e.g. rating and ranking mechanisms, comments and reviews. These activities and contributions play a central role in how the Web is used.

This chapter provides insight into web concepts that serve as a basis for the design and implementation of the **qKAI mashup framework** and the concept derived from it, which is described in detail in **Chapters 5** and **6**.

2.1 Web 3.0 and Social Media

Current web trends can be summarized under the term "Web 3.0" or "Social Semantic Web" [12], in which user-centered interaction is being intertwined with standardized data formats. First best practice applications, which are combining user interactivity with semantic data standards in a web context, are Twine [14], Freebase [15], DBpedia [16], and DBpedia mobile respectively [17].

The term "Social Media" is used as a synonym for "Web 2.0". Currently, the line between the Semantic Web and Web 2.0 is becoming much more fluid, allowing us to create new synergies in a Web 3.0 or Social Semantic Web environment. The combination of social user involvement, employing desktop-like interfaces with "rich user experience" (Rich Internet Applications or RIA [18]) and the Semantic Web with technologically oriented operability for data representation and processing, is a promising conceptual basis to solve two current problems:

- On the one hand, there is still a lack of lightweight user participation in Semantic Web contexts because hurdles need to be overcome and fancy interoperation ability is missing.
- On the other hand, there are claims for less trivial and more unitary content in Web 2.0 and Social Media contexts.

DBpedia [16] and Freebase [15] have started to address these issues by offering collaborative content collection, creation, and refinement, or semantic interlinking to increase freely available and distributed resources that can be interpreted successfully by humans and machines. Both integrate content from the online encyclopedia, Wikipedia [4] – currently the most famous community using wiki technology:

"Wikipedia is a free, web-based, collaborative, multilingual encyclopedia project supported by the non-profit Wikimedia Foundation. Its 16 million articles (over 3.4 million in English) have been written col-

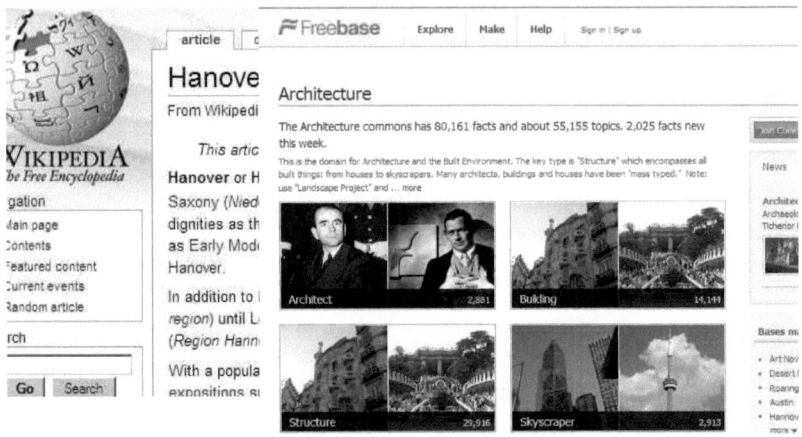

Figure 3: Example of a Wikipedia article about Hannover and a Freebase site about architecture in 2010.

laboratively by volunteers around the world, and almost all of its articles can be edited by anyone with access to the site." [4]

What all of the available solutions still have in common is a missing **knowledge-oriented focus** with emphasis on enhanced user interaction, incentive and motivation for interoperation and feedback.

The conjunction between virtual resources and real world resources currently happens, for example, by the principle of geocoding. Assigning latitude and longitude as geographical positions in real life allows interlinking virtual resources with real places, objects and persons. With the help of Global Positioning System (GPS) devices, localization and positioning of real resources becomes possible and traceable. Also virtual worlds and 3D environments reflect the real world as a digital simulation of real world tasks and situations.

2.1.1 Online Communities and Social Networks

The traditional understanding of a "community" was once mainly the local area or neighborhood, since villages or cities needed to communicate with each other and get information. Today, when we speak of virtual communities or online communities (network communities), the local vicinity is not that important anymore. Via the Internet, people can engage with each other in communities across geographical and cultural boundaries in different ways.

In the area of **intelligent media systems**, communities can be used in a supportive, advisory or informational knowledge capacity, which can in turn be integrated into a variety of thematic relationships and everyday life for counseling and help.

In particular, mobile communities can be used as a **ubiquitous reference** and as **active collections of knowledge**. Communities have a wide range of synchronous and asynchronous forms of communication (email, forums, chat, news boards, wikis, blogs, reviews, comments, content collections and grouping, short messages), which can be used effectively for interaction and collaboration in a community.

There are many communities with a leisure-oriented focus, but the number of communities that follow sober economic interests, specialist, or interest-oriented objectives is rising steadily.

In the existing literature, various categorizations of communities can be found, such as commercial, theme-oriented or method-oriented communities, depending on the nature of the community, its purpose and type of audience. Parent is often divided into the following three types of communities [20]:

- **Communities of Interest (CoI)**: communities that are formed from a common interest like hobbies or sports
- **Communities of Practice (CoP):** communities that are formed from a common problem like diseases or legal issues
- **Communities of Association (CoA):** communities that are formed from similarities, such as inhabitants of a particular city, a former school, or fans of a certain pop star

Current research projects are concerned with the combination of collective user intelligence and lexical or semantic data collections to arrive at the use of controlled vocabulary for tagging [16] [21].

"The importance of online communities is increasing steadily. There is a clear correlation between active participation in the Internet and active and passive membership in communities. Every year the experience of Internet users is increasing and therefore their use of virtual social networks and communities."

"According to the study 'European Communication Monitor 07,' by 2010 'Social Media' will be a mission-critical communications tool, more important than sponsorship, events or corporate publications. Online communities have become a successful business model; this is proved by the horrendous sums, which were offered for communities like Flickr or YouTube." [20]

Online communities as a source of collective information and knowledge, such as Wikipedia, as an amusing exchange of messages such as Twitter [19], or as communication and exchange tools such as forums or chats, have become indispensable. They are committed to the social web culture, which is described in the next chapter. The different types of communities and Social Media have huge potential as a counseling, assistance and exchange platform or as a source of support in everyday life.

Online networks are represented on the current web by "Social Networks," such as Twitter [19] to post short messages, Facebook to connect with friends [22], Last.fm to listen to music [23], Foursquare

2 The Web as Distributed Knowledge Base

to locate things and friends [24], LinkedIn for business contacts [25] or Dailymile to share sports training information [26].

Regardless of which term is used - Web 2.0, Social Software, Social Media, Social Networks - a high degree of associated **social interactivity** is typical for all of them. Interaction takes place as communication between users, but users are also actively involved in content creation, feedback and enrichment.

Common to all Social Media is that users exchange information and resources on these platforms. The social network is used to create content, i.e. "User Generated Content," (UGC).

"Social networks are slang for a form of network communities, which house technical web applications or portals." [27]

Web 2.0 and the increasing use of Social Media are changing the way people deal with information on the web. An increasing number of users are not only information consumers (consumer), but produce and publish their own content simultaneously (consumer = producer + prosumer). User generated content (UGC) with community feedback is widely used in the "Social Web." Interactive information and knowledge offers are comfortably available via Internet at any time and place (24/7). Web-based user interaction, like wikis in Wikipedia, forums, weblogs or games, lets distributed knowledge grow as an open information space. Statistical and empirical evaluations are also possible; in addition to interaction and communication components, Web 2.0 capabilities include evaluation mechanisms, tools for providing exchange and feedback, groups and support in documentation and education.

2.1.2 Folksonomies

A particular phenomenon within communities, which came about in 2003 with Del.icio.us [28], the social bookmarking application in Web 2.0, was the concept of folksonomy (folk + taxonomy), which are features that allow lay people to collectively classify and index con-

2 The Web as Distributed Knowledge Base

tent freely and collectively (social tagging). The totality of the tags of all users is known as folksonomy.

Here, users interact mostly in open communities and there are no set rules for indexing. Each newly assigned keyword, such as a photo or blog entry increases findability when searching for tagged contents. However, the disadvantages of folksonomies are clear; ambiguity, subjectivity, and small deviations in the associated tags (e.g.

Figure 4: Delicio.us [28] tags and Flickr images about the architecture in Hannover [4]

singular vs. plural or different languages) can diminish the relevance (precision) of results, since a specific controlled vocabulary is not required. Many resources in folksonomies are not found because there is a lack of relevant tags. Famous examples of folksonomies are Deli.cio.us [28] und Flickr [4] (see **Figure 4**).

2.2 Open Content

As mentioned in **Chapters 1 and 2.1**, there are many resources available on the Web, but should resources be used over and over again without any restrictions? A huge knowledge base that is available for reuse without complicated copyright restrictions is called "Open Content." Open Content in this work is defined according to the description of Open Knowledge in *"Defining the Open in Open Data, Open Content and Open Information"* by the Open Knowledge Foundation [29]:

"A piece of knowledge is open if you are free to use, reuse, and redistribute it."

The derived qKAI concept (cf. **Chapter 5**) adds processing differentiation between Open Content as raw input information and Open Knowledge, which represents qualified information that has been checked or enriched. The Semantic Web of Data and User Generated Content (wikis, communities or weblogs) grow in a structured, unstructured and semi-structured manner. DBpedia [16] offers an extensive knowledge base in Resource Description Framework (RDF) format [30] (generated from Wikipedia content), allows semantic browsing and detailed thematic inquiries with SPARQL [31] (compare **Chapter 2.3**) queries for refinishing and further assignment.

The aim of the Semantic Web is to provide unique descriptions of entities, their relations and properties on the Internet [30] according to a standardized formula. This is an example of a resource or "thing" if we are talking about the renewed "Internet of Things." Access to resources is always carried out using representations. One resource can have several representations, such as extensible Hypertext Markup Language (xHTML), Resource Description Framework (RDF) [30] [32], Extensible Markup Language (XML) or JavaScript Object Notation (JSON) [33].

Open shared databases like Freebase [15] offer a free Application Programming Interface (API) to reuse its content with its own Metaweb Query Language (MQL) [15]. Relational databases can be easily converted into Web of Data by embedding existing components like a D2R server [34]. Additionally, many unstructured sources like

HTML sites or PDF files do not apply to machine interpretable web concepts yet. Serializing this data to standardized formats with open access is the first step towards enhanced machine and user interpretability. Aperture [35] and Virtuoso Spongers [36], for example, enable comprehensive solutions for these tasks. In case more text engineering is needed, there are comprehensive solutions for standard Natural Language Processing (NLP) tasks (e.g. OpenNLP [37]) to perform sentence detection, NER (Named Entity Recognition), POS (Part-Of-Speech) tagging or even semantic chunking.

2.3 Linked Open Data (LOD) and Semantic Web

With the Linked Open Data (LOD) [38] community around DBpedia [16], a huge knowledge base in standardized and machine interpretable format is available, which represents a semantic representation of the Wikipedia online encyclopedia. Another advantage of LOD is that resources are extendable and reusable without copyright restrictions under the GNU license, in terms of "Open Content" and "Open Knowledge."

"DBpedia is an effort to publish structured data extracted from Wikipedia: the data is published in RDF and made available on the Web for use under the GNU Free Documentation License, thus allowing Semantic Web agents to provide inferencing and advanced querying over the Wikipedia-derived dataset and facilitating interlinking, reuse and extension in other data-sources." [38] (see **Figure 5**)

The Semantic Web, increasingly described as "Linked Data" [9] or "the Web of Data," is supposed to bring a new aspect to the Internet. What used to be known as internet pages for use by human beings only, will now be applied to automatic processes. In order to achieve this, the former will be classified as continuous text existent data and its properties will be transformed into defined forms, the aggregation of which will be connected through labeled links.

2 The Web as Distributed Knowledge Base

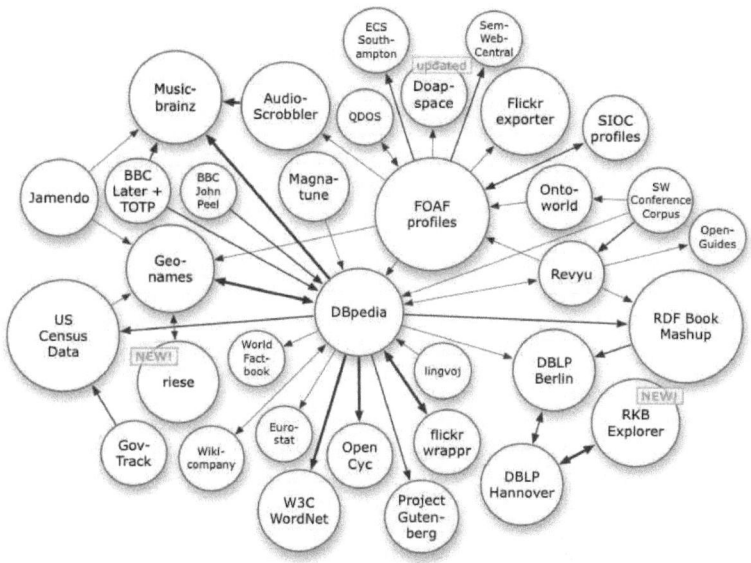

Figure 5: DBpedia Linked Open Data cloud [16]

The "Resource Description Framework," (RDF [30]), structure developed for this purpose follows a natural speaking sentence structure. It consists of the following information carrier: The "subject," "resource" or "node" is presented as a URI (Unified Resource Identifier), just like a "predicate" and "object." All of them might contain properties following their description. The properties themselves are typed and if we imagine RDF as a tree, they would represent the leaves. Their type is normally described, for example, as a number, like 42, which is of the type "integer," which is functionally dependent on its predicate. The relation of the information carriers is modeled implicitly and always directed and qualified through the predicate. Instead of speaking about subject, predicate and object (the object might be a subject as well), it is more efficient to name them "properties" that are assigned to resources. Resources are connected to relations in three ways relations: As source, target and identifier.

SPARQL

With SPARQL (SPARQL Protocol and RDF Query Language as recursive acronym) [31], a search and query language for RDF repositories was designed. SPARQL has been a W3C specification since the beginning of 2008. SPARQL's syntax is similar to SQL, which allows columns to be defined to answer requests. Filtering expressions are possible in SPARQL that are placed in the WHERE clause in SQL for example. Up to now, there has not been an efficient functionality to implement full text search. Aside from ASK, there are no aggregate functions available in the SPARQL specification at this time. ASK allows only a true/false statement about whether a request delivers a result or not. Abandoning the special case of identity, regular expressions should be used for full text search. Such expressions do not fit a large amount of data properly because there are still no database indices available to speed them up to text. That is why every expression for any RDF property has to be evaluated and all of the properties have to be fully loaded also. To get more aggregate functionality in addition to ASK, many providers use additional, proprietary extensions. These standardized extensions, which are not yet standardized, use the strength of the traditional, relational query language SQL and a combination of SPARQL and SQL. This is why qKAI does not use SPARQL by itself. Temporary query results have to be stored anyway to allow acceptable performance while requesting and combining distributed RDF resources. These results are stored in a MySQL relational database, and SQL is utilized for effective, internal data processing.

2.4 The Web Behind the Scenes – A Technical View

In the following, the techniques, which are seen as important in future web applications are explained in relation to the technology research done in conjunction with this thesis.

2.4.1 The Central Principle of Resources

A web resource is a virtual entity that is available for consumption by users to benefit from it. Web resources contain different types of content and formats like text or multimedia (image, sound or video). In the web context, every resource is identified by a name in the form of a Uniform Resource Identifier/Locater (URI or URL). This identification enables interaction and interlinking of distributed resources over the Web. One resource can offer different representations to suit the needs of different consumers like a machine or a human being.

The amount of valuable resources is enormous. There are several platforms and communities offering resources in every domain and format for nearly any purpose. Especially in Web 2.0 and Semantic Web, the amount of freely available and collectively created resources has increased. Overall, the Web offers many (free) available resources that should be utilized as a distributed knowledge base for interactive information exchange, learning purposes and knowledge transfer. The challenge is to facilitate, improve and simplify access, representation and user interaction regarding autonomous, distributed web resources.

A new generation of intelligent tools and services for interactive information and knowledge transfer, collaboration and learning has to be developed, which relies on semantically interlinked and distributed resources.

There are still no comprehensive application scenarios or enhanced user interaction concepts available in information and knowledge transfer that are **based upon existing web content**. Extensive web-based resources are available (most are open to the public), but are not yet embedded as **interactive knowledge bases** in higher-layered applications in information and knowledge transfer with sustainability and mutual benefits for all areas.

The challenge lies in **the utilization of existing web resources** through collaboration, standardization, modeling, and enhanced representation **instead of new content creation** to allow innovative user interaction scenarios in an incentive way with the web-based knowledge base available.

Linked Data Principle: Informational and Non-informational Resources

Here we find an interesting context, in which resources and how they are handled on the Web is discussed. In the following excerpt, H. Halpin and V. Presutti describe the classification of information and non-information resources in relation to Uniform Resource Identifiers (URIs):

"The primary goal of the Semantic Web is to use URIs as a universal space to name anything, expanding from using URIs for web pages to URIs for real objects and imaginary concepts,' as phrased by Berners-Lee. This distinction has often been tied to the distinction between information resources, like web pages and multimedia, and non-information resources, which are everything from real people to abstract concepts like 'the integers.' Furthermore, the W3C has recommended not to use the same URI for information resources and non-information resources, and several communities like the Linked Data initiative are deploying this principle. The definition put forward by the W3C, that information resources are things whose essential nature is information is a distinction at best." [39]

2.4.2 RESTful Web Services

Representational State Transfer (REST) [40] [41] is an architectural style in software design that is not tied to any particular technology, although it is used as a guide for designing system architectures that follow constraints.

2 The Web as Distributed Knowledge Base

Web services are *"software systems designed to support interoperable machine-to-machine interaction over a network."* [42] They are identified by an URI (Uniform Resource Identifier) and can be accessed via HTTP (Hyper Text Transfer Protocol) by using XML-based communications protocols like SOAP (Simple Object Access Protocol) or XML-RPC (Extensible Markup Language Remote Procedure Call). Web services greatly support the collaboration of applications running on different platforms because they abstract from specific programming languages and operating systems; and by doing so, constitute a type of distributed system.

Beside SOAP and XML-RPC, the REST architectural **style of web services** has caught the media's attention over the past decade. In his dissertation "Architectural Styles and the Design of Network based Software Architectures," Roy Thomas Fielding describes a style of software architecture comprised of distributed hypermedia systems, which he calls **Representational State Transfer**, **REST** for short. Fielding has designed this architectural style by starting with a "Null style" [40] that does not impose any constraints on those elements that are part of a system having the respective architecture and he then applies constraints that "differentiate the design space" [40] incrementally. Any service that complies with these types of constraints can, in a strict sense, be referred to as **RESTful**.

The Central Principle of REST: Resources

Wikipedia provides an excellent explanation of resource handling according to a REST architectural software style while developing web applications [41]:

"An important concept in REST is the existence of resources (sources of specific information), each of which is referenced with a global identifier (e.g., a URI in HTTP). In order to manipulate these resources, components of the network (user agents and origin servers) communicate via a standardized interface (e.g., HTTP) and ex-

change representations of these resources (the actual documents conveying the information). For example, a resource that represents a circle may accept and return a representation that specifies a center point and radius, formatted in SVG, but may also accept and return a representation that specifies any three distinct points along the curve as a comma-separated list.

Any number of connectors (e.g., clients, servers, caches, tunnels, etc.) can mediate the request, but each does so without "seeing past" its own request (referred to as "layering," another constraint of REST and a common principle in many other parts of information and networking architecture). Thus, an application can interact with a resource by knowing two things: the identifier of the resource and the action required, it does not need to know whether there are caches, proxies, gateways, firewalls, tunnels, or anything else between it and the server actually holding the information. The application does, however, need to understand the format of the information (representation) returned, which is typically an HTML, XML or JSON document of some kind, although it may be an image, plain text, or any other content." [41]

REST Constraints

Client-Server

In a client-server architectural style, a (reactive) server offers a set of services, which are requested by the (active) client. The principal behind this constraint is that the client and the server can function independently of each other. This improves portability of the client code and allows the server code to be simpler and therefore scalable, allowing the client and server to evolve independently from one another. [46]

Stateless

This constraint refers to the communication between a client and a server. This means that no client context is stored on the server, i. e.

each request from a client to a server contains all the information necessary to understand and handle the request properly and the client is responsible for storing all the stateful information.

Cache

This is a concept known from the World Wide Web, in which responses to requests may be cached on proxies to improve network efficiency. This concept is added as a constraint to clients, so that they can cache responses (given that they are cacheable) and reuse them as responses to suitable subsequent requests.

Uniform Interface

Interfaces between components in a REST architecture (in general, clients and servers) are uniform, which simplifies the overall system architecture. Components can evolve independently from each other as "implementations are decoupled from services they provide." [40] There are four constraints to interfaces, which are necessary in order to have a uniform interface in a RESTful manner:

- **Identification of resources:**
  Resources used in an interaction between components are identified by a unique identifier (e.g. a URI), and are separated from a particular representation, which enables different representations (HTML, XML or JSON) of the same resource and clients calling a resource may choose which representation to return.

- **Manipulation of resources through representations:**
  If a client has the appropriate permission, actions (delete or modify) on a resource only happen for the representation that the client currently holds by using the HTTP's uniform protocol (GET, PUT, POST, DELETE).

- **Self-descriptive messages:**
  Messages passed between components include enough information to enable receiving components to process or transform the contents of a message.

- **Hypermedia as the engine of application state:**
  Each server response (a representation of a resource) should

contain information about what actions a client is able to perform and this information is provided as a link-related resource.

Layered System

In a layered system, each component only sees the immediate layer it is interacting with, which means that it cannot see "beyond" this layer. This constraint reduces overall system complexity. Intermediate layers improve system scalability because they enable load balancing and shared caches, and may be used to enforce security policies.

Code-On-Demand (optional)

This optional constraint allows client functionality to be extended by downloading executable code from the server, e.g. in the form of Java Applets or JavaScript scripts. This constraint simplifies clients because it reduces the need to pre-implement desired functionality directly into them.

2.4.3 Elements of a REST Application

In **Chapter 2.4.2**, the REST architectural style for distributed hypermedia systems was introduced. The purpose of this chapter is to provide insight into an exemplary REST application, which illustrates which elements are involved, and the role they play. Code fragments used in this section are based on **JAX-RS** [43] (Java API [44] for RESTful web Services), or to be more precise, on its reference implementation, **Jersey 2** [45] [46].

Resources

Every resource in a REST application is identified by its Uniform Resource Identifier (URI) and clients are able to access those resources via their URI. A server responds to a request for a resource by returning a representation of the resource. The client and the server share the same meaning of the returned representation. A

2 The Web as Distributed Knowledge Base

typical resource in an online shop is a shopping cart, where customers can put in the articles they want to buy. **Listing 1** illustrates the definition of a shopping cart resource using Jersey [45] [46].

```
1  @Path("/shoppingCart/{cartID}")
2  public class ShoppingCartResource {
3      @GET
4      @Produces("text/xml")
5      public String getShoppingCart(@PathParam("cartID") Integer cartID) {
6          return DataProvider.getShoppingCartContentById(cartId);
7      }
8  }
```

Listing 1: Java based REST resource

The @-annotations in the resource definition have the following meaning [43]:

- @Path: relative URI path of the resource (relative with respect to the base URI of the hosting server)
- @GET: request method designator specifying the HTTP method that the annotated method will process
- @Produces: specifies which representation MIME3 types the resource can produce
- @PathParam: a parameter that can be extracted from the request URI and which can be used in the resource class

If a client wants to request a shopping cart, a GET request to the host server must be invoked. In this example, the request URI is comprised of the base server URI hosting the requested resource, the relative URI of the resource as defined by the @Path annotation and an ID of a shopping cart, so the GET request in this example would look like this:

GET http://onlineshop.com/shoppingCart/1234

Representations

2 The Web as Distributed Knowledge Base

The @Produces annotation defines the MIME types that a resource can produce, e.g. JSON4 [33], HTML or XML. In the example above, the resource produces an XML representation of a shopping cart and this representation may look like the illustration in **Listing 2** [46].

```
1  <?xml version="1.0"?>
2  <shoppingcart xmlns:xlink="http://www.w3.org/1999/xlink">
3      <customer xlink:href="http://onlineshop.com/customer/1234">1234</kunde>
4      <position nr="1" amount="5">
5          <item xlink:href="http://onlineshop.com/item/25" nr="25" />
6      </position>
7      <position nr="2" amount="2">
8          <item xlink:href="http://onlineshop.com/item/74" nr="74" />
9      </position>
10 </shoppingcart>
```

Listing 2: XML representation of a REST resource

This example representation clarifies an important property of REST architectural style, which has been presented as a constraint to the uniform interface, and that is **hypermedia as the engine of application state**. The returned representation contains links to other resources, which the client may access and by requesting those resources, the client transfers from one "representational state" to another [33] [40].

Methods

Resources created with Jersey's reference implementation [45] can be accessed using the standard HTTP methods GET, POST, PUT, DELETE and HEAD. The shopping cart resource, for example, can be processed via GET requests as defined by the @GET annotation in **Listing 2, line 3**. Via POST requests, clients may extend resources with further content, e.g. by adding new items to a shopping cart. New resources, like a new shopping cart, can be created by the PUT method and an existing resource can be deleted by using the DELETE method. The HEAD method is equal to the GET method except that it does not return the body of a response [46].

2.4.4 Rich Internet Applications (RIA)

Regarding today's browser-based user interfaces, most Rich Clients use asynchronous JavaScript and XML (AJAX [46]). The aim of Rich Internet Applications (RIA [18]) is to bring desktop-like and easy-to-use interoperation to the Web. Next to AJAX [47], Adobe Flash/Flex [48] and Java-based User Interfaces (UI) are technical alternatives. The best technique to choose depends on the main requirements that have to be fulfilled. Flash/Flex3, for example, offers the advantage of less scripting work and easier event handling to reach highly interactive functionality if the focus is on multimedia and design issues. All these Rich Clients can be seen as an extended and enhanced view in the traditional Model-View-Controller (MVC2) concept. Advantages of the Rich Clients offer are faster reaction to user requests with partial reloads of site parts without refreshing the whole site, less network traffic and server load, as well as being able to work offline. A Rich User Interface (RUI) Engine delivers the General User Interface and the presentation logic is separate from the visualization components. RIAs as stand-alone web clients that interact with the server side through web services are a promising combination. One of the most important advantages of the Client-Server model is the idea that the User Interface should be developed independently of the business logic and data persistence technology.

Nevertheless, in today's web programming practice before RIAs, the UI is in fact tightly coupled with the server-side technology of choice. If you want to change your backend functionality from Java to PHP, you also have to rework all the scripts generating the HTML user interface (UI) from *.jsp to *.php. To avoid this problem, you can now choose a Rich Client, which communicates through standardized interfaces like web services only and put most of the UI logic on the client side to get a true separate solution.

2.5 Summary

In **Chapter 2** insights into current web technologies and concepts are presented. The Web is regarded as a distributed, partially free, available and rich knowledge base delivering Open Content (as an example). The central principle of resources, users and interaction between them is interpreted by the semantic annotation of resources following Linked Data principles and Representational State Transfer (REST) constraints.

RESTful web services can be interpreted as an adapted, utilized representation of a resource or a resource collection, respectively. Web services can aggregate distributed web resources (e.g. querying, modeling, representing or annotating them) and interacting with the users. The basic principles of RESTful application are shown in **Chapter 2.4.2**. The derived qKAI mashup framework for web applications presented in **Chapters 5** and **6** is based on the REST software architecture style. Therefore, it is introduced rather than explained in detail.

3 The Convergence of User Interaction and Game Design on the Web

Game design principles are finding their way into other fields like advertising, marketing, learning software or social web applications with increasing frequency. The reason behind this trend is simple; people love to play games. Games manage to keep users motivated for a longer time than other activities, because they do not perceive playing as something they have to do; it is something they like to do. This, of course, only applies if the game follows properly incorporated game design principles. Obviously, fun is a great motivator [49]; therefore, it is natural that users would be attracted to areas other than game design if they think it will be fun.

By applying simple game principles to other types of activities, like reward points to a "boring" vocabulary trainer, the vocabulary trainer becomes a vocabulary learning game. Students or other users of such (and other) learning games stay motivated and learn quickly because they do not perceive it as learning, but playing. Companies use Advergames to promote their products on the Internet. Whereas banner ads are something that most users feel uncomfortable with, Advergames have the ability to pique user's interest and this is a basic requirement for customer acquisition. For (social) **web applications** like Flickr [4] or YouTube [5], **motivated users are essential** because they create the (open) content that is presented to users and without such content these web applications would be "unviable." It is therefore no surprise that web applications tend to use game design principles to keep their users motivated. In this thesis, a meta- rewarding system will be presented that rewards users for any kind of interaction/activity within any kind of web application.

For this purpose, a **global interaction rewarding model** (GIAR) has been designed which classifies typical activities within web applications and rewards those activities with points and special awards. The meta-rewarding system is implemented via RESTful web services, which executes two tasks: activity logging and rewarding, and generating activity stats, which are known from game design (user rankings, level progression, etc.) [46].

3.1 Interweaving Gaming Principles with Web Applications

Since the first days of the World Wide Web, web design process has been developing continuously. The first available websites presented the user with static content; today, users are able to create new content interactively. Web design has evolved into web application design, where the internet browser acts as the operating system and websites act as the applications with which the user interacts. As websites become more and more interactive, principles and methodologies known from interaction design (id) must be considered during the design process of a web application. One basic principle is that there is not "the" solution to a known interface design problem; there are always more solutions. Therefore, designing interfaces is always an iterative process of building prototypes and testing them with users to validate or dismiss a solution [50].

In the past few years, a new trend can be observed in popular web applications like Twitter [19] or Flickr [4], in which game design principles are used to motivate and encourage users to keep active within their applications. The great benefit of games is that people enjoy playing them (for hours or even days) because it is fun; it is something they like to do since "playing is something one chooses to do." [51]

More and more web applications make use of **simple game mechanics** like collecting points or providing leaderboards to "put the fun in functional" [53] and by doing so, users are kept motivated since they perceive the application as a game and have fun using it.

3.1.1 Interaction Design and Gaming Mechanics

Designers of modern, interactive and engaging websites must incorporate tenets from the previously mentioned disciplines, such as **web design, interaction design and game design** into their websites. Incorporating even simple game mechanics like rewarding points, leaderboards or level systems causes significant overhead during the design process of web applications. One has to choose which interactions to reward, and develop algorithms and models for leaderboards or level systems and compute activity statistics for users.

In *Games People Play*, E. Berne defined games as a series of interactions [59]:

"A game is an ongoing series of complementary ulterior transactions progressing to a well-defined, predictable outcome. Descriptively, it is a recurring set of transactions... with a concealed motivation... or gimmick."

"To re-state Berne's definition, one can think of a game as a series of interactions (words, body language, facial expressions, etc.) between two or more people that follow a predictable pattern. The interactions ultimately progress to an outcome in which one individual obtains a 'payoff' or 'goal. In most cases, the participants of the games are unaware that they are "playing."'

Data management efforts increase as the need to manage the content that users create interactively also increases. Creation of **interactive content** is still the main purpose of web applications, as well as providing the data needed for applied game mechanics. In some cases, the work involved in applying game principles does not pay off, e.g. for short-term online surveys where the main purpose is to aggregate data. Especially for these kinds of applications, the quantity of data is important and this can only be accomplished by motivated participants.

The **quality of data** is crucial for applications like the qKAI mashup framework, which utilize information based on Open Data for interactive knowledge transfer. Assessing certain criteria regarding the quality of information can hardly be managed automatically because these criteria are subjective. Therefore, it is up to motivated users to contribute information about such criteria.

Utilizing game mechanics without the need to integrate them into an application can be achieved by using an independent global interaction rewarding service that deals with the whole "game" management. One only needs to choose which interactions to reward and integrate corresponding service calls into the application to be developed. The service manages interaction logging and rewarding, the evaluation of activity stats like leaderboards, level rankings and other kinds of information that have the ability to encourage people. The rewarding service acts completely independently of a specific web application and can therefore aggregate activities within the different applications that a person is actively using. This can be used to derive some kind of a global "WWW-activity" ranking that reflects how active users are on the internet and could motivate them to become more active in the various web applications in which they have accounts.

3.1.2 The Competition for Attention and Feedback

One main problem regarding user interaction in web-based applications and systems is how to motivate users to engage in ongoing interoperation and to build compelling and addictive scenarios with incentive and rewarding. Without the adequate ability to user interaction, available resources remain useless for the end user. Particularly in the area of Social Media and Online Communities, we can talk of **competing** for the **user's attention,** ongoing **participation** and **feedback**.

In all managing disciplines regarding information, learning or knowledge management, gaming principles are becoming more and more important in motivating users to participate continuously and to get users to deal with learning material in a more incentive way.

On the one hand, there are solutions that deploy gaming for content enrichment ("Games with a purpose" [54]); there are also solutions that deploy gaming for learning and there are some gaming mechanics adapted in the interaction concepts of Web 2.0 applications. A combination of these approaches remains to be seen. In this thesis, they will be combined and adapted to web-based, knowledge-oriented scenarios related to distributed web resources to gain the advantages inherent in each approach.

In addition to the simple fun factor, game-oriented user interaction is suitable for several tasks in web applications, knowledge engineering and learning:

- To transfer knowledge and to learn (especially fact-related knowledge)
- To bring ongoing incentive and motivation to participate in web applications
- To deduce new information about a resource and its interacting user (enhance content)

There are still no connections between these different areas. Combining them could have advantages and create symbiosis in all areas. This will be shown by example during the course of this thesis.

Gaming mechanics have just started to be interwoven with web applications in Web 2.0. Online communities like Flickr [4], Foursquare [22], Dailymile [26] or Amazon [55] embed interaction design components from game design to increase motivation, incentive and participation. In other words, we can talk about "Functional Fun," while combining gaming mechanics with useful tasks like learning or enhancing content.

Games are introduced as **interactive knowledge systems** in this thesis (see **Chapter 5**). This means a knowledge-oriented derivation of the concept "Games as systems of information" by Salen and Zimmermann [56]. Gaming mechanics are well suited as an aid in the many steps involved in knowledge engineering, e.g. annotation, evaluation, acquisition or representation (see **Chapter 4.2**).

The concept of this thesis aims at embedding distributed resources to turn them into gaming content to simplify access and to enhance ongoing motivation to interact. Every kind of user interaction with a resource brings new information with it (inference and feedback) about the quality of the resource or the interoperating users themselves. Therefore, **every activity in relation to a resource** can be stored and traced in connection with the interacting user and the interaction task to allow further processing and analysis.

The game industry is commonly known as the most challenging field regarding hardware and software requirements or technical challenges. New input devices, interfaces and sensors are often developed for gaming purpose (WII games console). Complex, but fast algorithms are needed to manage demanding tasks in real time even for multiplayer scenarios. The technical requirements for gaming have to be excellent on the client and server side, if we think about web-based multiplayer games like World of Warcraft (WOW) [57].

Game-based interaction can be seen as a **highly sophisticated form of user interaction**. High design and high functionality are necessary to motivate users to continue playing a game.

Current user interaction design in the area of social web applications shows a convergence between traditional web interaction and adapted game mechanics (e.g. Flickr [6], Amazon [55]). For example, leaderboard functionality is established to increase user participation and motivation. Collecting, points, feedback, exchange and customization are some of the primary principles in gaming that can be useful for interaction design in web applications. Basic gaming mechanics in web applications can serve as a tool to keep up the user's motivation to continuing participation and feedback.

In social web applications the first aim is to get the user's attention and then enable the user to interact with content and other users. The next important aim is to get **resonance** or **feedback** by the user and about the user. Without any response, the users' attention would remain useless in a community. From this it follows that an important question in social web application design is, how to persuade users to give active and immediate feedback. Here, we find another common aspect between web applications and game design: feedback is a crucial part (see **Chapter 3.2**).

C. Crumlish says the following about the relationship between game design and social applications [58]:

"The fascinating intersection between game design and social design that's opening up new possibilities for social experiences in game environments and introducing playful elements to social interfaces. An application doesn't have to literally be a game or be presented as a game to employ many of the same design techniques that make games fun to play.

It's no coincidence that Ludicorp's first product was something called Game Neverending (their second was Flickr, which owes at least some of its success to the almost addictive game like quality of its user interfaces). Even in the enterprise, interfaces don't have to be dry and tedious. Think about how to delight your users and encourage them to engage with each other.

Games are among the oldest 'social interfaces.' The rules and tokens of a game provide a set of affordances and an environment in which people interact. In fact, people will make up their own games with whatever elements they find handy. Many of the 'memes' that spread on sites like LiveJournal, blogs, MySpace, and Facebook ('Which Buffy Character Are You?' '37 Things You Didn't Know About My Cat,' or 'iPod Shuffle Ouija') utilize built-in posting, commenting, and polling features, which isn't to say that you couldn't encourage your users to invent games for each other by giving them generative tool with which to do so."

3.2 Game Design Characteristics

Compared to the first existing computer games like Pong [60], developing (good) games today is a complex process. It may take several years from the initial idea to developing a market-ready product and often involves staff members playing different roles within an organization, e.g. producers, publishers and developers [46]. The development process itself may also be comprised of several stages like pre-production, production, milestones and post-production [61]. It would go beyond the scope of this thesis to address the game development process as a whole. The main purpose of this chapter is to provide insight into the subtask of game design in game development. According to Wikipedia, game design is "*the process of designing the content and rules of a game in the pre-production stage and design of game play, environment and storyline during the production stage.*" [62]

Therefore, the first two stages of game development deal with game design, whereas the milestone stage deals with the development of ascending game versions like alpha, beta and the final release version. The post-production stage deals with game maintenance after it has been released. Before we take a closer look at game design, it must be mentioned that the forenamed game development process and its components are just a generic sketch of how to create games and can be found in (most) game developing companies. It varies from company to company and from game to game, as it depends on the game type/structure/concept itself, the company's size and its experience with game development. The chosen procedure is a good way to create games for example in qKAI (cf. **Chapter 5 and 6**) and many other purposes as well, especially in the Social Media and web application areas. [46]

Before elaborating on the game design process, we need to take a closer look at some of the general characteristics of a game because some of these characteristics raise issues that game designers need to think about during the pre-production stage [46].

First, it must be noted that the terms game and play are used synonymously. The word play, however, can be seen as a hypernym of the word game, but this thesis will not go into the details of the relationship between play and game.

One characterization of play comes from the Dutch historian, Johan Huinziga, who was a supporter of the homo ludens (Latin: "playing man") explanatory model of human beings, which states (among other things) that humans evolve their skills through playing [63]. In his principal work, *Homo Ludens*, he identifies the following characteristics of play [64]:

1. Free activity.
2. Outside "ordinary" life.
3. Follows fixed rules.
4. Creates excitement and fun.
5. Limited by a certain time and space.
6. Has no material interest or profit.
7. Has (intrinsic) goals.

Based on these characteristics, we can derive (at least) five degrees of freedom available to game designers: time and space, goals, rules, excitement and fun, and escape from "ordinary" life. In his book, *Digital Game-Based Learning*, M. Prensky sums up and specifies these degrees of freedom and its higher characteristics into the six key structural elements that most (computer) games have [65]:

Rules can be seen as a kind of a map that forces the players "to take specific paths" while playing because they limit the number of possible interactions a player can have in a certain situation and since they hold true for all players playing the game, rules make a game fair. While for most non-computer game rules are explicitly written down and managed by the players themselves or a third party like a referee in a tennis match, in computer games rules are built into the game and players learn them interactively by playing the game.

Goals are important for motivation in games (and in real life) because human beings are a goal-oriented species. The basic goal of games is to win, for example, by defeating the final enemy or having the highest score. However, a player can have many other goals, like reaching a high level, collecting rare set items or solving a tricky puzzle. Even "goal-less" computer games like a flight simulator or the Sims [68] have goals, even if they are not so obvious. A goal for a flight simulator game could be a successful landing and within the Sims, it could be a goal to reach a "happy" mood for a Sims character.

Outcome and Feedback provide players with a way of keeping track of their progress in regard to their goals. Computer games, in particular, use feedback to let players know if their interactions they have a positive or negative effect. Positive feedback, for example, means that a player is getting closer to his or her goals, whereas negative feedback may indicate that a player has broken a rule, which usually moves him or her further away from set goals. There are several options for "implementing" feedback: a numerical value representing a score displaying the total number of points earned, charts with bars displaying the player's current level and progress, virtual characters in a game that a player can talk to, and newer technologies like the Wii remote 5 use haptic technology to give tactile feedback. Feedback is a crucial part of games because through feedback players learn how the games work., Computer games make extensive use of feedback, especially with in-game tutorials, whose purpose it is, to explain how the game is played and the features of the game. However, one has to keep in mind that providing the right "amount" of feedback is essential to a player's playing experience. Too much feedback may disturb the course of the game and the player may become stressed out. If the playing experience stops being enjoyable, the player will certainly not return to the game. Not enough feedback may also result in frustration for the players because they will not understand the effect of their interactions, which results in a diminished, playing experience. Ideally, the amount of feedback presented to a player should be adaptive, keeping in mind the player's current stage of development. [46]

Challenges are a part of most computer games and a player has to take them in order to improve himself as a player or the character in the game. Challenges can be against another opponent like a "real" player in a Massively Multiplayer Online Role-Playing Game [66] (MMOPRG) or an "artificial" player in an action game like Devil May Cry [67]. Challenges do not necessarily need an opponent; in a simulation game like SimCity [68], a typical challenge is to reduce unemployment by building enough industrial and commercial areas. The difficulty level of a challenge should always match a player's skills and this adaption is a key feature in game design, which is called "balancing."

Balancing aims to keep a player in a certain mental state is called flow, a concept introduced by Csíkszentmihályi [69]. In this "flow" state, players are fully concentrated on their current challenge. Their ability to solve the challenge matches the challenge's degree of difficulty almost perfectly. They feel neither anxious nor bored and they can master the activity at hand easily without any stress and with pleasure. The chart in **Figure 6** illustrates the **concept of flow**. It is the relation between the skills of a player and the difficulty level of the challenges to be solved over time.

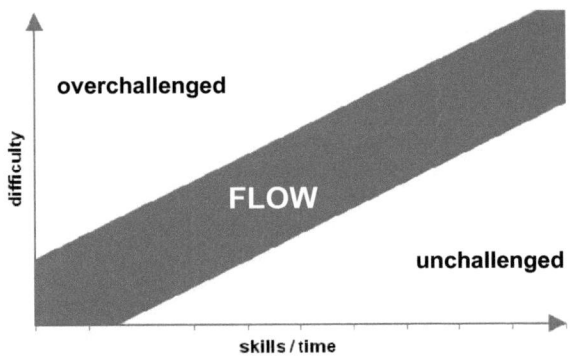

Figure 6: Flow in games [69]

If a challenge is "above the flow," a player will certainly get frustrated because the task is too difficult to solve and therefore motivation decreases. On the other hand, if a task is too easy to master, a player may not feel challenged enough and motivation decreases as well. This concept of flow can also be partially transferred to learning scenarios. Learning aims also cannot be too difficult so that the learner does not become frustrated and therefore not finds it easy to reach the state of learning new things [46].

Interaction must not only be seen as something that happens between a player and a computer, it also has a social aspect because many games are played with other people. This of course holds true for almost all non-computer games, since the number of single player games is small compared to games played with others. With the World Wide Web, designers of computer games are increasingly including social interactions into their games. There are very many MMORPGs [66] available and probably the most successful of them is World of Warcraft [57]. Critics that say playing computer games is an isolating activity need to be aware of the fact that most computer games today involve social interactions, even though these social interactions are not face-to-face. This brings up the question of whether restricting social interaction solely to computer games results in another form of social isolation. This is something that should be examined more closely. [46]

Representation refers to the fact that games have a theme and therefore contain narrative elements revealing the "story" of a game. Whereas some games have a pretty simple and obvious "story" like Tetris [70], which is about "building and recognizing patterns" [71], other games, like the very successful role-playing action game (RPG) Sacred 2 [72], have a polished storyline that accompanies the player throughout the game. Surely, the type and complexity of a representation depends on the design of the game. Regardless of whether a game is direct or indirect, abstract or specific, every game "is about something" and game designers need to think about how to incorporate narrative story elements into the game that clearly explain what the game is about. [46]

3.2.1 Basic Game Mechanics

Games use different mechanics to create an enjoyable game play. While there is probably not one complete list containing all the possible mechanics available, there are five game mechanics that have been brought together by Amy Jo Kim [73], which have proven to be useful not only for games, but also for interaction designers creating social software and web services.

Points

Rewarding user interactions with points or something similar is a basic, yet very effective mechanic that almost every computer game uses because they are easy to integrate and may serve as a basis for a host of other mechanics. Points may be used to assemble leaderboards, which have great motivational potential because they tap into people's "innate competitive drive" [74], however game designers need to be aware that leaderboard mechanics encourage people to "game the system," which colloquially means that they learn how to achieve the highest rankings. Another application of points are levels that map a user's in-game progress or experience, for example, role-playing games use levels to unlock new powers or items. Beyond the game industry, points are often used to strengthen customer loyalty by making them redeemable, e.g. Payback [75] (Germany) [46].

Collecting

Collecting is very popular and not just with computer games. People collect just about anything: shoes, baseball cards or stuffed animals. When it comes to computer games, people collect weapons, trophies or set items. Completing a set is a highly emotional moment because it often takes a long time to find all the set items and sometimes this never happens, which is frustrating to most players. Collecting mechanics generally have a high engagement factor because people are happy when they discover or gain things, especially in applications or games with a social background because people love to brag about their collection.

Feedback

The definition of feedback by A. J. Kim [73] as a game mechanic is the same as M. Prensky's definition of feedback as a structural key element (**Chapter 3.2.3**): Feedback is the basis of a player's progression. If a game does not provide any feedback on interactions by a player, she does not know how these interactions affect her progression or the game play itself. In addition to this functional aspect of feedback, according to Amy Jo, feedback also makes the game "more fun and compelling" [74].

Exchange

According to A. J. Kim's definition, "exchanges are structured social interactions," [74] which can be explicit or implicit (in other words emergent). For example, most massively multiplayer online role-playing games provide options to trade items socially with other players and this trading interaction is explicit. A typical implicit interaction, mostly known from social browser games like Farmville [76], is called "gifting," which means that one can give others a gift of items they have earned or found.

Customization

Almost every game offers the possibility to customize it, starting with the graphics resolution or the volume of the sound effects. In addition to technical customization, players are also able to change their in-game character's look, attributes and equipment. Customization may be performed automatically, e.g. by testing a graphics card's performance or adjusting the graphics resolution, or by the players themselves, e.g. by changing the color of a car in a car racing game. [46]

3.2.2 Reward Types

Game designers make great use of their imagination when it comes to incorporating engaging rewards, since there are is no limit to the types of rewards possible. The following partial list introduces some of the typical rewards that can be found in one form or another in most modern computer games [77] [46].

3 The Convergence of User Interaction and Game Design on the Web

Figure 7: Sacred 2 skills [72]

Skill Rewards are used to enable players to improve their in-game character's attributes and/or skills, e.g. increasing strength and vitality like in Sacred 2 [72] (**Figure 7**), or anything else that can be enhanced, e.g. technologies in Civilization [78]. This is usually accomplished by rewarding skill points that players can freely distribute to the different skills and/or attributes that they possess.

Inherent Rewards are not directly assigned by a game; it is the game's inner workings, like graphics or sound that players enjoy, assuming that the game has a good design. Things like a thoughtful, exciting story or an imaginative, virtual world can be very rewarding,

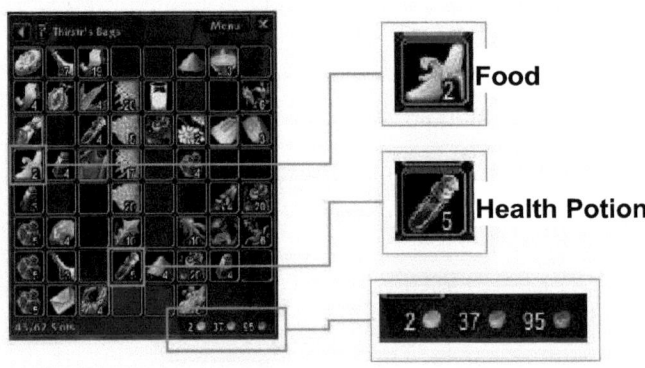

Figure 8: World of Warcraft inventory [57]

3 The Convergence of User Interaction and Game Design on the Web

which can also enhance the player's experience.

Resource Rewards can be found in games where resources play a role and this reward type can easily be included. Typical resource rewards are in-game currencies like gold or coins or resources that are "essential for survival," like food or magic, health potions and other types of resources that are required by the game itself, e.g. armor and weapons. These resource rewards can usually be collected and stored in an inventory (**Figure 8**). [46]

Extension Rewards are assigned if a game can end due to time limitations or because characters die. The game rewards extra time or extra lives to extend the time a player can spend playing it. A widely known example of extension rewards are the green "1-up mushrooms" used in Super Mario Bros [79] to extend Mario's number of lives (**Figure 9**).

Accomplishment Rewards, in general, are challenges a player accomplishes in a game. Accomplishing typical tasks in games, like

Figure 9: Mario's 1-Up Reward [79]

leveling up, beating an enemy or finishing quests, can be rewarding if the degree of difficulty matches a player's progress, otherwise they are too hard or too easy to handle. Motivational Rewards are simple things like points or trophies that a player can earn or win, but they are not only confined to virtual goods. In-game characters can also provide encouragement with words like "well done" or deeds that may be very motivational to players.

3.2.3 Preproduction

As mentioned before, the game design process is comprised of two design stages, the preproduction stage, where a game vision is developed, and the production stage, where the game vision is filled with life and translated into program code. This section focuses on the preproduction stage because the concepts and methods used in this phase are independent of the type and purpose of the game to be designed; and can also be used in other contexts (see **Chapters 3, 5.2, 6.5 and 7.1**).

Every game design process starts with an initial idea or rough outline of the game to be designed, which becomes more specific during the pre-production stage. Game designers use a central document also referred to as game design document, which maps the whole design process and serves as a resource for the later design stages, especially the production stage. As mentioned before, the design process is iterative. Therefore, the game design document is constantly subject to change. It is not rare for the release version of a game to differ totally from the one described in the game design document. Translating a game vision into specific terms means dealing with several questions that typically arise during the game design process. In the following, we will take a closer look at a few of them [46].

What is the genre of the game?

In most cases, the genre of a game is determined by idea at the beginning of the design process. According to M. Prensky, eight game genres exist and every game falls into at least one of them [80]:

- Action
- Adventure
- Fighting
- Puzzle
- Role Playing

3 The Convergence of User Interaction and Game Design on the Web

- Simulation
- Sports
- Strategy

Who is the target audience?

This question is certainly less important for people who design and develop games in their free time. For game design companies, it is crucial to define the target audience because they want to sell their product successfully, so the more they know about their audience, the better they can fulfill their needs. Besides ethnic, social and media aspects, game designers must also consider the personal preferences of the target audience, since every player has their own understanding of what constitutes fun and excitement. The designers of Multiplayer Online Games (MOG) often make use of the Bartle Test to qualify a player's gaming preferences. This test was developed by Richard Bartle, a British game researcher. The test classifies players of multiuser dungeon (MUD) games into four groups [81] [46]:

- **Achievers** — their main desire is to gain points and reach higher levels
- **Explorers** — their goal is to explore and discover as much as possible within and about the game (internal things like game quests and functional things like bugs)
- **Socialisers** — their main interest is to interact or communicate with other players
- **Killers** — they look for challenges and seek conflict with other players.

The four player types exist in differing relation to each other. The number of different group members influences overall behavior. For example, decreasing the number of killers would increase the number of socializers.

What are the Game's Aesthetics?

Roughly speaking, game aesthetics are about the look and feel of a game, and many factors have an influence on this. The first thing that comes to mind when thinking about the aesthetics of a game is graphics, which is very important because this is what a player perceives first. However, other factors particularly influence the feel of a game. Rules are "at the heart of a game" and "control how a game is played" [82]. They determine what a player can do and how it can be done. If rules are not balanced, (e.g. in terms of fairness), a player leaves the "flow" state (see **Chapter 3.2.1**) and does not perceive the game play as fun anymore. Perspective has an effect on how a player experiences the in-game environment, e.g. the first-person perspective provides less of an overview of the surroundings; on the other hand, it may present a more intense playing experience than the third person perspective. When it comes to the number of players, game designers need to choose whether to develop a single player or a multiplayer game because this decision mostly has an impact on other parts of a game. Rules, especially, must be adapted or added to handle situations with multiple players playing at the same time and in the same space. While there are many aspects regarding the aesthetics of a game, these are just a few that need to be considered [46].

What are a Game's Mechanics?

A. J. Kim, an experienced designer of games and social networks, describes game mechanics as a *"collection of tools and systems that an interaction designer can use to make an experience more fun and compelling"* [73]. In other words, game mechanics revolve around creating an enjoyable and engaging playing experience. There are plenty of mechanics available, but which mechanics a game designer should or should not incorporate into a game depends on the type of the game, since some of them might not be appropriate. Furthermore, currently available game mechanics are

3 The Convergence of User Interaction and Game Design on the Web

not the measure of all things, although some of them have been in use for a long time and are still useful. Game designers are constantly seeking new mechanics that create fun, particularly because the possibilities for interaction between a player and a game or between players have changed in the past decades. Compare, for example, the first Pong [60] game, where the only possible interaction was to move the paddle up and down, to the latest Wii [83] games, where players may use their hands, feet and voice. Obviously, there is a relationship between the game's mechanics and its aesthetics (as described in the previous section) because game mechanics have a deep impact on how a game makes players feel. This relationship was developed by Marc LeBlanc [84] in a concept called MDA (Mechanics, Dynamics and Aesthetics), which states that mechanics induce dynamics based on player interactions and this in turn invokes emotions (aesthetics) in a player. There are two perspectives of this concept, which are illustrated in **Figure 10**: the designer's perspective and the player's perspective. Game designers start with creating rules (mechanics) that lead to a dynamic behavior system, which trigger specific aesthetics. [46]

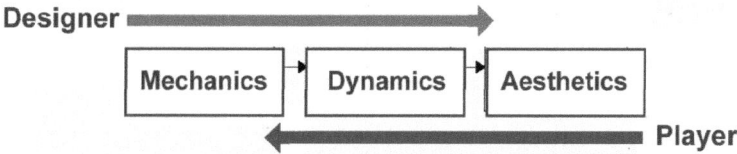

Figure 10: Mechanics — Dynamics — Aesthetics concept (based on [84])

With a view to applicability in other contexts, **Chapter 3.2.1** gave an overview of basic game mechanics that are not only useful for computer games, but can also be used in other applications where user engagement plays an important part.

Which Types of Rewards Should be Incorporated?

Rewards can be found in almost every game (in one form or another), they can be tangible like a trophy or less tangible like a compliment [77]. Independent of the type of reward, however, they all have one thing in common: They (should) make a player feel positive about receiving the reward and by doing so, enhance the play experience. This may sound easy to accomplish, but game designers need to be aware that the positive effect of a certain rewarding mechanism always depends on a player's personal preferences. While some players feel positive and engaged by a certain type of reward, others may be annoyed. In this case, the rewarding mechanism has an opposing, negative effect on the play experience. One may think that a higher number of rewards correlates with a better play experience, but in fact, if a game offers too many of them, possibly without the need for a player to do something for them, the positive effect of being rewarded decreases because at some point there will be nothing to get excited about anymore. Then again, if players are rewarded too little, motivation drops and playing the game becomes a chore. Therefore, providing the right type and number of rewards is one of the challenging subtasks of game design. A selection of the reward types that are typically used in game design is introduced in **Chapter 3.2.2**.

How do Players Track Their Game Progress?

This is an aspect already mentioned in **Chapter 3.2.1**. If players can progress by earning points, winning rewards or mastering challenges, the game must provide some kind of stats visible to a player, so that he is able to keep track of his progress. Many games provide stats in the form of a level-system, where points or other units are mapped to a level value that displays a player's progress. Level systems are a very powerful way to engage people; in most games that use level-systems, reaching a high level is equivalent to having more strength and the benefits or attributes that follow from that, like being able to wear stronger armor, fight with more powerful weapons or use rare items. In general, stats that represent a player's behavior have the ability to change that behavior, at best in a positive way [46].

3.3 Games with a Purpose: Social and Educational Gaming

L. v. Ahn's reCAPTCHA, ESP game [85] or Amazon Mechanical Turk [86] established gaming as a well-suited instrument to solve several tasks in knowledge engineering. However, they do not address any learning or knowledge concerns while gaming. Users can enrich content, learn and share knowledge through gaming with Open Content in a way that is challenging and creates social incentive. We aggregate and enrich existing information while interacting with Open Content. In short, activities like creating, editing, rating, ranking, interlinking and grouping content are assignable to gaming tasks.

The idea of combining social networking, gaming and rating is not new. Nevertheless, there are no applications available in this area that focus strongly on knowledge and learning. Present social games do not rely on standardized Open Content or sustainable concepts. Gaming content is manually created for every single game. Generic approaches to building an ongoing social knowledge network based on available content are still missing. So far, there has been little discussion about embedding gaming into superior learning structures regarding learning management standards, e-learning infrastructures and the Internet of services. Different from other gaming approaches, content creation itself, is part of our game-based concept. Players acquire the ability to change their view of relevant resources. For example, text and multimedia is presented as extracted chunks of information or images. These **knowledge snack** concepts are supposed to enhance understanding and portion out information, so as not to overload the user. Sections of articles are presented to the user, so he has to guess the context;

sights are presented in detailed zoom view to let users figure out what they are; and locations are placed on the right position on a map so the user sees where they are.

Luis van Ahn introduced crowd sourcing and content enhancement to gaming together with ESP game or reCAPTCHA [85]. Guess-the-Google [87] is a term guessing game based on Google search results or images. Scoyo [88] offers a game-based learning platform for kids, but does not deal with Open Content or Open Access. In general, there are no generic game-based concepts available that take web standards and knowledge engineering into consideration that are based on distributed resources, like Open Content (The Open Knowledge Definition [89]). There are some commercial, social gaming applications, like Playfish [90], MegaZebra [91] and Zynga [92], that have an informal character. They are often embedded into Web 2.0 platforms like Facebook [22] or MySpace [93] to increase participation. BrainGame [94] offers commercial offline knowledge games and learning adventures with static content.

3.3.1 Educational Aspects and Suitable Domains

Gaming, overall, is not suitable for learning any skill in any domain. Some educational tasks and topics can be learned and transferred more effectively by certain gaming types than others. Further, content has to be divided into different difficulty levels and tasks for distinct audiences. Our game-based concept is not limited to a certain audience. Game creation is a gaming and learning challenge in itself. Lecturers can choose suitable content out of the gaming pool and add their own material or other web resources, if necessary. In general, every domain seems to be suitable for our social educational gaming approach if learning aims can be fulfilled while creating, answering and querying factual information, as well as predefined learning tasks (especially recall and rearranging factual content).

Popular examples are multiple-choice questions, text-text assignments, image-text assignments or ordering questions. These question types have the advantage that they are also available as learning standards in Learning Management Systems. We can easily convert them into IMS/QTI [95] after in-game creation. Embedding multimedia like zoom parts out of images or video/audio sequences is also possible. As an example, next to knowledge-unit gaming types, location-based gaming types can rely on geocoded information and correct geographical placement.

3.3.2 Game-Based Learning and Knowledge Games

Game-based learning is created to provide both education and pleasure. Playing relaxes people and makes them more receptive to learning. Controlling the game flow may be stronger in educational games [96]. Competence is stressed via feedback mechanisms. Educational games should look and feel like traditional computer games from beginning to end [51]. Open Content is a huge knowledge base, however augmented interaction abilities used to confront users with Open Knowledge little by little, in an enjoyable manner (knowledge-snacks, casual games), are missing. We are looking for mechanisms that bring more motivation and incentive to the user, while interoperating with Open Content. Therefore, we chose a game-based learning approach embedding Open Content in knowledge games.

"In most academic subjects 'content' below the most advanced level is relatively standard, and therefore fungible. And so as future students pore over reviews on web sites and in magazines, voting course-by-course with their dollars, it will be the courses' Game play and its accompanying motivation – not the content – that will be the deciding purchase criterion...." [51].

Gaming is not suitable to learn any skill in any domain. Some educational tasks or topics can be learned and transferred more effectively by utilizing certain gaming types over others. Furthermore, content has to be divided into different difficulty levels and tasks for distinct audiences. Our game-based learning concept is not limited to a certain audience.

The following domains seem to be the most suitable to embed for further evaluation purposes because of the huge amount of available Web resources: Geography, architecture, history, events, persons, medicine and health. Overall, every domain seems to be suitable for our social educational gaming approach if learning aims can be fulfilled while creating, answering and querying factual knowledge and predefined learning tasks (especially recall and rearranging factual content).

Especially in the area of learning and working where motivation is a crucial factor since motivated students and employees are more productive and less stressed [51]. There are many learning games for children available that enhance how they learn, since they can learn more easily and without any resentment. Other examples of combining fun and learning are various famous TV programs for children, like Sesame Street or Nickjr on the Nickelodeon network where children learn how to count or recite the alphabet in a playful manner.

3.4 Gamification

Web (application) design, interaction design or social educational games are not the only domains where fun and other game principles are used to create engagement. Embedding gaming mechanics in daily life situations and non-game applications particularly consumer-oriented web and mobile sites, in order to encourage people to adopt the applications is known under the term "Gamification".

"Gamification works by making technology more engaging, and by encouraging desired behaviors, taking advantage of humans' psy-

3 The Convergence of User Interaction and Game Design on the Web

chological predisposition to engage in gaming. The technique can encourage people to perform chores that they ordinarily consider boring, such as completing surveys, shopping, or reading web sites." [98]

Famous examples of Gamification are introduced by Volkswagen in 2009 under the name "The Fun Theory" [52]. The Bottle Bank Arcade Machine[4] for example turns everyday tasks like bottle recycling into fun. Evaluation results showed up twice as many users with gaming mechanics added.

Figure 11: Bottle Bank Arcade [52]

Figure 11 shows the Bottle Bank Arcade setting where the bottle recycling container is turned into an Arcade game with points as incentive for every bottle inserted. Flashlights are indicating in which hole to insert the next bottle to gain points. Therefore, Volkswagen's

---

[4] http://www.youtube.com/watch?feature=player_embedded&v=zSiHjMU-MUo, update: 2009, visited: 2011-05-12.

slogan was "*Can we get more people to use the bottle bank by making it fun to do?*"

3.5 Summary

The convergence of game mechanics, interaction design and web applications is currently a hot topic, but one that still presents some challenges for web developers and interaction designers. With Social Media the competition for the user's attention, attendance and feedback plays a very important role and can be regarded as the motivating force of social communities and online marketing strategies.

Game mechanics and Gamification are increasingly finding their way into social web applications – sometimes quite obviously, such as by using a point or badge system. Collecting, feedback, exchange and customization are some of the most feasible game mechanics that can be adapted to web application activity. Incentive in relation to ongoing activity is very important and can be reached by badges and further in-game awards in the first step. Regarding the long term, getting virtual badges only might get boring, so other types of awarding concepts are necessary.

In the following we take a closer look at the impact of Social Media on knowledge engineering in **Chapter 4**.

4 Social Media and Related Changes in Knowledge Engineering

The availabilty of Social Media has changed the way we handle requested resources and how we operate with each other on the Web. New challenges in the area of knowledge engineering have arise like how to query or embed Social Media into knowledge management concerns effectively. In addition, interactivity and the focus on interaction between users and resources in Social Media contexts create new ways of enriching and annotating content collectively following the wisdom of crowds and helpful intelligent automatic analysis.

4.1 Social Media as a Knowledge Source

As shown in **Chapter 2,** the Web can be regarded as a distributed knowledge base with valuable resources like texts, pictures, videos and audio files for any purpose. There are different use cases possible for integrating distributed web resources into knowledge management and engineering applications. All applications have one thing in common — they need mechanisms that motivate users to interact with available resources. An initial pool of web resources has to be ready for exploration and inquiring by users. We have to offer a starting point to the World Wide Web and its endless, constantly growing resource possibilities (querying DBpedia [16] and using Linked Open Data concepts [38]).

Query languages like SPARQL [31] are very helpful in acquiring relevant distributed resources. Most of the Social Media flood is not structured semantically, however Linked Open Data offers a good starting point because of its ability to be queried by SPARQL, and interlink non-semantic resources as well.

4.2 Knowledge Engineering

The goal of knowledge engineering (kn) is to present complex expert knowledge in intelligent information systems. Next to representation and visualization of the acquired and remodeled knowledge, user interaction and activity play an important role with regard to knowledge engineering issues in modern web applications, especially social software and online communities. Interactivity and user experience in web applications have reached new dimensions and win user's over with their desktop-like applications, in terms of ease of use and richness of feature richness.

The creation of personal and adaptive views of knowledge is also a knowledge engineering task and it is useful to explore wide knowledge bases. Knowledge engineering influences user interaction concepts here by affecting information flow and the presentation form of the desired knowledge.

Knowledge engineering is a sub-area of knowledge management (km), which aims to depict knowledge in knowledge-based systems or expert systems. In the past, content was explicitly created by experts in traditional knowledge engineering processes and stored in closed databases and knowledge bases. Standard tasks of knowledge engineering include the **acquisition, formalization, representation** and **visualization of knowledge and information**.

Chapter 3 introduced basic gaming principles and interweaving with the web application domain. Gaming can also be useful for knowledge engineering tasks, as this thesis will outline in **Chapters 5.1** to **5.3**. Game-based tag ranking is one example of enhancing the quality of the content by user activity. Resources are acquired, annotated and represented as model for effected knowledge engineering tasks. In addition, users' activity and output should be considered, while analyzing, engineering and modeling knowledge from web resources.

4.3 Social Impact

Web 2.0 or Social Media has brought a new dimension and change to knowledge management and engineering, (e.g. wikis and weblogs). Today, anyone can become an author for web-based content and the distinction between producer and consumer has become more fluid and moved towards a "Prosumer" mentality. A new kind of open collaboration, knowledge collection and sharing has emerged. This also means greater access, variety and distribution of knowledge and information. Personal opinions and subjectivity play a big part in weighing the influence of content and its collective relevance and importance. The effect of "The Wisdom of Crowds" has found its way into knowledge engineering and information processing.

The problem of **contents quality** arises if someone can declare himself an expert in a specific area, however, the state of the art, regarding the Wikipedia community, for example, shows that the mechanisms of social and collective control are working very well. A comparison of Encyclopedia Britannica [97] and Wikipedia showed that they are both similar in quality [99].

Web 2.0 mechanisms can be helpful for new concepts in fulfilling the **knowledge life cycle** and its single tasks. Users can be involved in the standard tasks of knowledge engineering in a collaborative and collective way ("hybrid intelligence"). User interaction tasks can be mapped to these knowledge engineering tasks. Some of the ways that a user's interaction can help is to create, edit, annotate, evaluate or qualify knowledge and information resources. The web is on its way to becoming a global, distributed and all-embracing knowledge base for nearly every purpose and domain.

4.4 The Issue of Quality

As we have seen in the last sections, the quantity of web resources is not a problem. The Web offers autonomous and frequently useful resources in a growing manner. User Generated Content (UGC) like wikis, weblogs or webfeeds often do not have one responsible authorship or declared experts who check the created content for accuracy, availability, objectivity or reliability. The user is not able to control the quality of the content he receives easily. If we want to utilize the distributed information flood as a linked knowledge base for higher-layered applications (e.g. for knowledge transfer and learning), information quality (iq) is a very important and complex aspect to analyze, personalize and annotate resources.

In general, low **information quality** (iq) is one of the main discriminators of data sources on the Web [100]. Assessing information quality with measurable parameters can offer a personalized, smart view on a broad, global knowledge base.

If we want to embed web content into information and knowledge transfer, the issue of data quality is unavoidable. Information quality is an important concern if we want to build knowledge out of information to use it for educational purposes. Currently, web users are clamoring for content that is more sophisticated, and less triviality [101]. Utilizing autonomous web resources by qualitative assessment is becoming more and more important.

To let users interact with Social Media and Open Content out of distributed web resources, enhanced inquiry, selection, storage and buffering are important prerequisites. Nevertheless, statements about the resources' iq enhance its fitness for use. **The more we know about a resource, the better we can reuse it.** As part of the qKAI mashup framework, we implemented the "qKAI hybrid data layer" for acquiring, storing and representing Open Content out of distributed resources. In qKAI,

4 Social Media and Related Changes in Knowledge Engineering

During this thesis, Open Content is boosted as an inherent part of higher-layered applications in knowledge and information transfer via standard tasks of knowledge engineering and augmented user interaction. Especially regarding smart user interaction, we have to offer user interfaces with high scores in certain information quality criteria. If we find out about a resource that contains Chinese text by analyzing its metadata, we can deduce that its understandability is most likely not ideal for European users. There are many small indicators and functions, which are very helpful in assessing and enhancing the information quality aspects of Open Content. In the following, we introduce the meaning of information quality exemplified with selected criteria. The relation between these criteria, qKAI data interaction issues and Open Content is explained.

4.4.1 Assessing Quality of Information of Autonomous Web Resources

"Information quality is one of the main discriminators of data and data sources on the web. ... The autonomy of web data sources renders it necessary and useful to consider their quality when accessing them and integrating their data." [100].

Information quality is often described as "fitness for use" [102] in the literature. Metadata plays an important role for the determination of iq-criteria. To a great extent, information quality is subjective, because we have to mention multidimensional criteria while assessing context, user and task dependence. Subjective dimensions of iq must be assessed by the help of user interaction [100]. User interaction can be basic, direct or indirect feedback.

"Many iq-criteria are of subjective nature and can therefore not be assessed automatically, i.e. independently and without help of the user." [100]

Because iq is often subjective, task and context-dependent user interaction plays a very important role while assessing subjective iq-criteria. To let users rate and rank content according to certain iq-criteria, questionnaires are widely used.

4.4.2 Information Quality Criteria and Open Web Content

Fitness for use may depend on numerous factors like actuality, believability, completeness or relevance. Not all single criteria can be assessed independent of each other [103]. Next to several other properties, the most important criteria of information quality in web applications are actuality, reputation, believability and accuracy of content.

In contrast to processes inside of enclosed organizations that analyze iq as a cyclic management task, the assessment of iq in the Web relies on autonomous information providers in an open information space. Therefore, in web-based systems iq is assessed by the help of user interaction to determine the "fitness for use" of an information source for the specific task at hand [103]. Social aspects of iq, especially in the context of Web 2.0, are reputation and trustworthiness of the author.

Important for the believability of information is the reputation of the creator. Every user has his own opinion based upon own experience or the experience in his knowledge circle. All experiences that are made with resources in qKAI are logged in history protocols. Different opinions about the reliability or trustworthiness of single actors regarding certain themes emerge. Personalized knowledge views can be deduced this way.

There are trust metrics and policies for **reputation-based systems** available in the literature and research [104] that can be implemented next to **interaction-based** and metrics that **rely on metadata**.

4.4.3 Categorizing Information Quality

The categorization of information quality can be found in the literature available according to various criteria and dimensions [105]. We did not find out much about generic interaction components to assess ongoing iq in web-based knowledge systems by online assessment [95] components with game-based features. We see the combination of reputation-based and global metrics as an especially promising first step towards an incentive and motivating way to assess iq sustainability.

Table 4 shows the iq citeria and their classification for autonomous information systems [103]. The iq criterion accuracy is defined as the percentage of data without data errors, such as non- unique keys or out-of-range values. Mohan et al. provide a list of possible data errors [100].

Accuracy is interpreted in a biased way in qKAI: On one side, we have to assess the data accuracy, on the other side we speak of semantically and syntactically correct information.

The last one can only be assessed by enhanced user interaction of experts or collective intelligence approaches (Wisdom of crowds).

Category	Criteria/Dimension	Objective/Subjective
Intrinsic criteria (Independent of the user's context)	Accuracy*	objective
	Consistency	objective
	Objectivity	objective
	Timeliness	objective
Contextual criteria (Context, task and user dependent)	Believability	subjective
	Completeness	subjective
	Understandability	subjective
	Relevancy	subjective
	Reputation	subjective
	Verifiability	subjective
	Amount of Data	subjective

Representational criteria	Interpretability	subjective
	Rep. Conciseness	subjective
	Rep. Consistency	objective
Accessibility criteria	Availability	objective
	Response Time	objective
	Security	objective

Table 4: Iq citeria and their classification for autonomous information systems based on C. Bizer's categorization [103].

4.5 Related Work

Wang [106], Naumann [100] and Bizer [103] et al. offer comprehensive research work about categorization, definition of information quality and related vocabulary in the domain of web-based information systems. Wikipedia [4] has its own quality assessment deploying a review mode by authors. Freebase [15] allows the user to rearrange, connect, correct or annotate available resources. Rating, ranking and recommendation at Amazon [55] are feasible examples of enhanced user interaction to qualify content. Flickr offers properties related to a picture that enable to rate a photo's quality. Tagging allows users to restructure and weigh their knowledge in a self-controlled way. Revyu [107] allows the users to rank and rate everything. The existence of available interlinked context information (e.g. in other web applications) is a first and simple step in determining the information quality of resources according to scores (relevance, reputation, popularity).

On the one hand, users can enrich content in a game-based way; on the other, users can learn and share knowledge through gaming with Open Content in a social incentive and challenging way. We are aggregating existing information and enriching it while interacting with Open Content. Even statements about the content's quality can be deduced out of users' content and activity. Fact-related knowledge, especially, can be transferred and learned if resources are presented in a rule-based manner to the user and if he has to solve predefined learning tasks to earn rewards.

There are games available to enhance content and there are games available that concentrate on learning. However, the idea of games with a focus on knowledge engineering and transfer that are based on Open Content and enhance the content's quality as a side effect of recent user interoperation is new so far.

4.6 Summary

Social Media has changed the attitude of web users from passive consumer to active participant and creator. Collective opinions, ratings and rankings weigh content in a collaborative and democratic way. The wisdom of crowds entered the web with communities like Wikipedia, Flickr and YouTube. The user remains in the center of social communities. Interactivity is ubiquitous, diverse and simple with different devices like notebooks, smart phones or sensors.

The question of the content's quality is more important than ever because of the vast information flood generated by various users and often non-experts in the social web. Information quality criteria like relevance or popularity are used as a tool to better reuse qualified Open Content in the qKAI mashup framework as outlined in **Chapters 5** und **6**.

A global interaction reward model that is independent from single web applications and can be extended in a generic way is still missing. Among others, this thesis aims to construct a meta-rewarding system to reward user activities like editing, login, creating, commenting and so on, in a global and standardized way as outlined in **Chapter 5.2**.

5 qKAI Concept: Utilizing Distributed Web Resources for Enhanced Knowledge Representation

In this chapter, we outline what we see as a prerequisite to turning distributed resources on Open Content into an organized, useful knowledge base for higher-level applications. We are aiming at the establishment of powerful mechanisms for acquisition and inquiry of relevant data out of distributed sources that are easy for the user to handle. We have to serialize formats for unitary, comprehensive analysis and mediation of distributed, inconsistent content. Mediation here means utilizing input data for higher-layered applications by offering personalized query plans, transformation, annotation and interoperation. Open access to knowledge and data (e.g. RDF representation) has the advantage of interlinking and accessing distributed data on the Web easily. Data processing concepts allowing machine and human-interpretable staging without storing redundant data permanently become possible by semantic interlinking.

Based upon the concept described in this chapter, we developed the **qKAI mashup framework** (qualifying Knowledge Acquisition and Inquiry) - a service-oriented, generic and hybrid approach combining knowledge related offers for convenient reuse (cf. Chapter 6). As part of the qKAI mashup framework, we implemented the **qKAI hybrid data layer** (cf. Chapter 6.4) to acquire, store and represent Open Content out of distributed resources.

Knowledge life cycle concerns can be matched with content cycles of the ReadWriteWeb. Acquiring (inquire, discover, categorize, index), maintaining, mediating (manage, analyze, enrich, transform) and particularly reusing (interoperation for information, learning, knowledge transfer) services have to be established.

Metadata and its annotation are essential for accurate thematic, semantic analysis and quality determination. Determining the quality of content enables us to rearrange it according to source criteria like provenance, timeliness or correctness. Emerging qualitative valence of information units and sources raises information to valid knowledge. To make the emerging qKAI knowledge base applicable, interaction services for learning, rating, ranking, inquiring, exploring and annotating, are needed. Motivation and user involvement are important aspects and learning games are well suited as easily accessible, intuitive forms of interactivity. Synergistic effects between learning, gaming and annotating content arise. Content enrichment by the user is seen as an implicit, positive side effect in qKAI mashup services.

5.1 Open Content in Interactive Knowledge Systems

Open Content is regarded as a distributed knowledge base in qKAI as mentioned before. Based on this data set, qKAI builds interactive systems (described in **Chapter 7**) to let users interact differently and better with the resources available and the other users involved. In qKAI, web-based games are interpreted as one example of

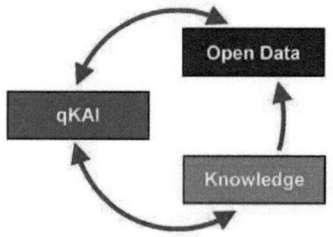

Figure 12: qKAI Open Data and knowledge cycle

interactive knowledge systems that rely on activity with distributed resources and other users. In particular, the Linked Open Data cloud outlined in **Chapter 2.3** offers an excellent knowledge base that interacts within interactive knowledge systems. **Figure 12** illustrates the conceptual role of the **qKAI mashup framework** by mediating between Open Data and content and knowledge management aspects like knowledge engineering or transfer.

The **qKAI mashup framework** is a **knowledge engineering framework** for distributed web resources and enhanced user activity with these resources. qKAI offers exemplary web services for various knowledge engineering tasks like querying resources, analyzing and enriching meta data, representing the resources formats, visualizing content, offering user interfaces with qualified resources and so on. qKAI concentrates on embedding DBpedia as Linked Data set relying on the wide Wikipedia knowledge and Flickr as exemplary image source.

5.1.1 Semantic Resource Annotation: A Global Knowledge Base from Distributed Resources

The classic World Wide Web consists of an accumulation of documents with information that dodoes not adhere to any structure. Given these circumstances, it is not possible for computers to decipher the meaning of this information. In order to enable computers to help users acquire and process the information overload of the World Wide Web, semantic annotations have to be added to the origins of the information. By means of this semantic metadata, information and meaning derived from different sources can be linked forming a global network of knowledge; this is also referred to as a **Giant Global Graph** or **Linked (Open) Data Cloud**. During the course of time, scattered semantic data sets and knowledge bases have been established. Their data can be identified using Uniform Resource Identifiers, which are accessed via HTTP and can be linked to other knowledge bases and resources via URIs. The open access Linked Open Data Cloud allows use of the network for its own applications. In many cases, it is desirable to be able to extend the resources of the network with custom semantic annotations. In this work a concept and web service to annotate resources of the Linked Data Cloud are developed. Applications that make use of this web service are discussed.

One of the objectives of this work is to develop a web service that provides the client with the possibility of annotating existing distributed semantic resources to expand the information of the semantic web to their own semantic information. This process is also referred to as semantic annotation. There are no standard procedures for linking resources to the metadata (annotations), rather, it depends on the application, which in this case would be based on the web pages (= resources):

- In the embedded annotation, the metadata is embedded in the document.
- For the internally linked annotation, the information source is linked to an external document, in which the semantic annotations are listed.

If annotations cannot be embedded in the annotation of resources because there is no write access or the format does not allow the annotations, the externally linked annotations are used. In this case, the semantic annotations are saved in an external document and the connection between the resource and the annotations will be made through a link outside of the resource.

For the annotation of distributed resources, the embedded and internally linked annotation is not a solution. The distribution of the information of a resource to several independent resources with restrictions to read access and without write access, only allows the externally linked annotation as a suitable annotation method.

5.1.2 Example of qKAI Resource Annotation

The resource "Hannover" is represented in several knowledge bases. For instance, one contains many pictures, another contains many facts, and others contain specialized geographic information on the resource Hanover. Now if you want new semantic annotations to provide or save this resource, none of the information/knowledge bases would be suitable for this project. None of these knowledge bases can be accessed as an outside end user/client or developer to add additional semantic annotations. We must therefore use an externally linked annotation — a new resource (same entity) outside the other knowledge bases to create references in their description/quantity statements of other knowledge bases/sources of information with the ability to add their own annotations. If you could visualize this result, it would look like the depiction of this process in **Figure 13**. This corresponds to an externally

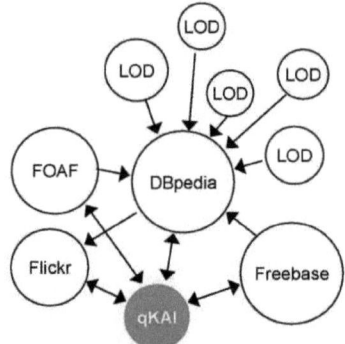

Figure 13: qKAI and LOD cloud

linked annotation process by adding a new node in the Linked Open Data Cloud, which creates a crucial difference to the already existing nodes (= knowledge bases and information sources) or the Cloud: This node provides the ability to add annotations. If one imagines the Linked Open Data cloud as a big database, you have this new hub with write/management access.

These findings are important for the realization of the qKAI resource annotator. They are a rough description of the concept that the qKAI resource annotator uses to enable semantic annotation of distributed resources. **Figure 14** illustrates the entity relation model for the qKAI resource annotation.

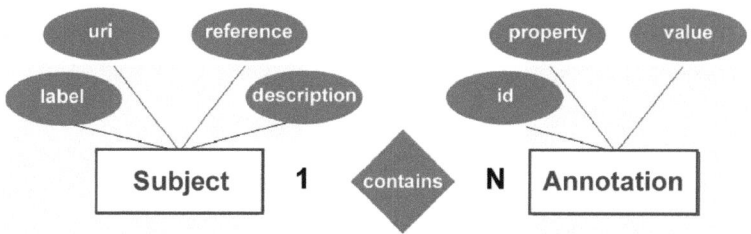

Figure 14: Entity relation diagram for the qKAI resource annotation

5.2 Rewarding Mechanisms and User Interaction

5.2.1 Global Interaction Rewarding (GIAR)

In qKAI, we reward any kind of web-based user interaction with a resource to increase user participation and incentive. This thesis proposes a **global interaction rewarding** service that rewards users for any kind of interaction in any kind of web application. [46]

5.2.2 Social Interaction Taxonomy

We can derive certain conclusions about users and the resources they use from a user's attitude toward his interaction with resources and other users. Therefore, a generic model (taxonomy) of interaction tasks in social web applications has to be designed and structured by type and purpose. Examples of possible interaction tasks are editing, creating, annotating, rating or ranking. For every interaction, the user should earn a reward (e.g. points) according to a global point and level system like in game-based scenarios. User-related interaction tasks can be stored to build knowledge-based user reputation or profiles. Every resource and every user can build their own transaction and interaction protocol this way. In the next step, the emerging protocol can be statistically evaluated to enable automated ranking and rating of users and resources. Inferences about interaction related criteria regarding the quality of information, such as relevance or popularity will be possible in the future.

An interaction taxonomy has been designed that classifies typical interactions in social web applications by type and purpose. Based on this taxonomy, a system of rewarding has been designed that rewards interactions with points based on the effort it takes to win them. As part of the rewarding system, a level and skill ranking has been designed that reflects a user's activities within different interaction classes and skills defined in the taxonomy. Besides points, users may win awards depending on the number of times certain interactions have been executed and the rewarding system regularly determines the most active users within interaction classes and skills and rewards them again with special rewards. To overcome the aforementioned need to integrate game mechanics into a web application, a RESTful web service has been designed and implemented that enables any kind of application to reward users for being active by simply calling the rewarding service. The web service provides two types of service calls: calls for interaction logging rewarding and calls for activity stats known from game design (leaderboards, level and skill rankings, progression and gained awards). Furthermore, a social web application has been designed and implemented where users are able to keep track of their logged activities, their current level rankings and progression, awards they have won so far and it enables users to compare themselves socially with other users.

5 qKAI Concept: Utilizing Distributed Web Resources for Enhanced Knowledge Representation

In order to create a global rewarding system that rewards users for any kind of interaction, interactions currently available in web applications need to be aggregated. **Figure 15** illustrates this aggregation via a Social Interaction Cloud that makes no claims of being complete because it is almost impossible to catch all interactions

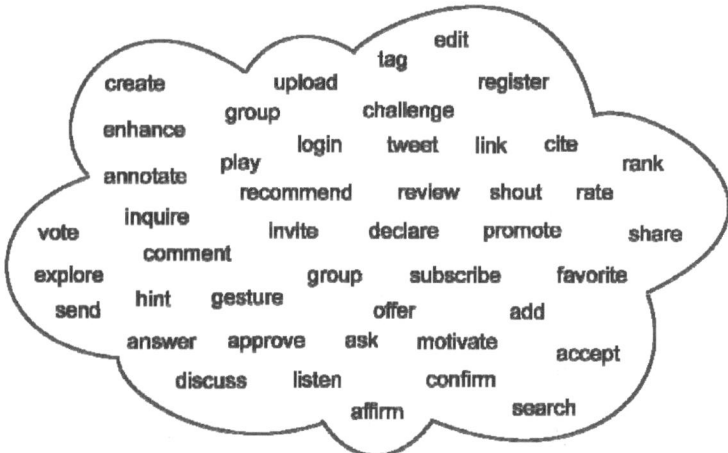

Figure 15: (Social) Interaction Cloud

from every available web application. In my opinion, however, the taxonomy that will be deduced in this chapter is generic enough to cover all possible (social) interactions and can therefore serve as a basis for a global rewarding model. [46]

Certainly, (social) interactions can be classified in various ways. The taxonomy deduced here classifies interactions using two consecutive criteria that are based on two questions. The first question is, **who is involved in an interaction?** Since the purpose of this thesis is to design a rewarding model that rewards user interactions, and every interaction involves a user, so a more precise question to ask would be, **with whom or what does a user interact?** The last question reveals which possible counterparts and interactions this taxonomy may have. It may either be a virtual object, like a video or a picture, which we will refer to as a resource; or, it may be another user, which in this sense, would constitute a "real" object. Therefore, the first criterion used to classify interactions initially, is whether it is a **user-resource** or a **user-user** interaction.

In the following, the first criterion will be stated more precisely by defining, what constitutes a resource or a user that is part of an interaction [46].

Criterion 1: Interaction Classifed by its Opposite Interaction

Criterion 1 classifies an interaction by its counterpart, which can be a resource, a user or both.

Resource: Resources are things like videos, pictures or blog posts, and in most cases, they are directly accessible via an URI. Otherwise, they are indirectly accessible via the web application hosting the resource. Resources do not have the characteristic of being "active" in an interaction, i.e. they are completely passive. Therefore, a user somehow interacts "on" and not "with" a resource.

User: Although users can be seen as a type of resource, we make a distinction between users and resources because users have the characteristic of being "active" in an interaction. In the sense of the previous definition, a user interacts "with" a user and therefore those interactions can be referred to as communication between users.

Both: In general, the purpose of taxonomy is not to classify an object into just one category, since an object may belong to different categories; some interactions may be classified according to both categories. For example, the grouping interaction may refer to group resources, such as in the social tagging system, GroupMe! [108]; or it may refer to a group of friends in the user-defined friend lists within Facebook. The result of applying the first criterion on the given interaction cloud is illustrated in **Figure 16**. It splits the cloud into two in-

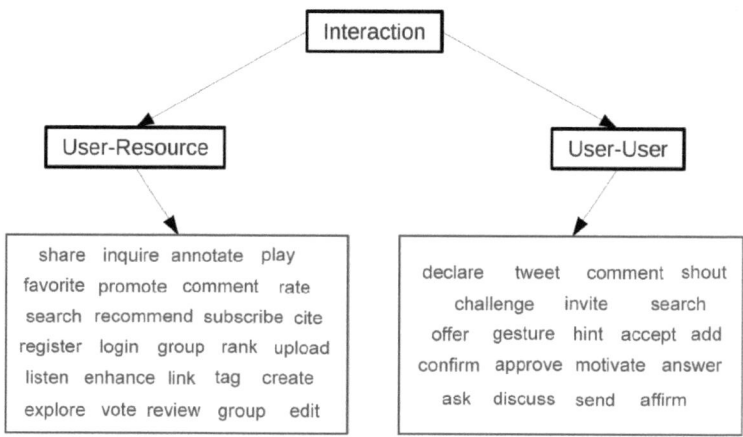

Figure 16: Interactions classified by its counterpart [46]

teraction-classes: the user-resource interaction class and the user-user interaction class where a user acts as a counterpart.

Criterion 2.1: User-Resource Interaction

Criterion 2.1 typecasts user-resource interactions by what a user does with a resource.

Create: Creating new resources means to make them directly or indirectly available via URIs. If a user uploads a picture to an online photo sharing community, the picture was available before, but not on the Internet. In contrast, if a user creates a new blog post, he "really" creates a new resource. Indirectly available refers to scenarios where a resource is protected and can only be accessed after authorization.

Edit: These interactions virtually "happen" around existing resources and do not necessarily result in a modification of a resource's contents, e.g. tagging a picture does not change it, but all these interactions are related to the edited resource.

Rate: Every direct or indirect, positive or negative feedback on resources is covered by this interaction type. For example, a book review is a direct rating, whereas subscribing to a GroupMe! group would be considered an indirect rating.

Explore: This interaction type covers all those interactions that do not fall into the previous types because, to put it crudely, nothing "happens" with a resource, it is neither created, edited nor rated, it is just explored. For example, if a user plays an online game, she explores it, but does not change it. The typecast of user-user interactions roughly follows the principles of the science of communication because it regards these interactions as communication between users. These communicative interactions are divided into two communication types and this distinction is based on how intense the communication is. In an intensive communication, sender and receiver switch roles constantly or at least once. The intention of a sender is always some kind of reaction by the receiver and this is not always given in less intensive communication scenarios where a reaction by the receiver is not always expected or even desired.

The intensity of a communicative interaction is the last criterion that typecasts user-user interactions into the following two types (**Figure 17**).

5 qKAI Concept: Utilizing Distributed Web Resources for Enhanced Knowledge Representation

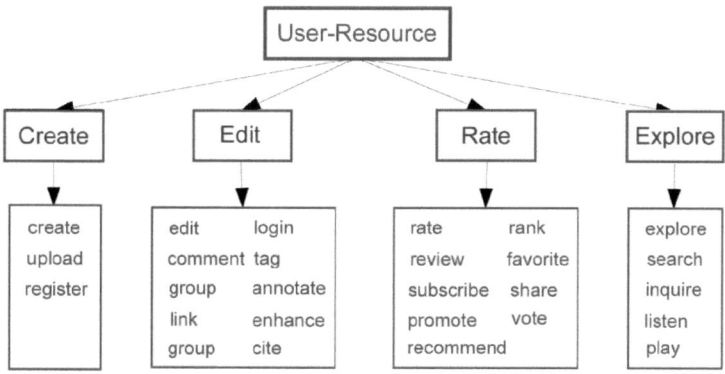

Figure 17: User-Resource interaction-types [46]

Criterion 2.2: User-User Interaction

Criterion 2.2 typecasts user-user interactions by communicative intensity.

One-Way: The sender is significantly more active than the receiver in a less intensive communication process, and for the most part, does not get any response from the receiver. This is why we refer to these interactions as being one-way because there is either no reaction required from the receiver or the reaction is not of any relevance to the sender.

Two-Way: A two-way interaction, as its name implies, is intensive communication, since both sender and receiver are active and constantly switch roles in the communication process. Even if sender and receiver only switch roles once, for example in a scenario where a user asks a question that is answered by another user, it is of high relevance for the sending user to get a response from at least one receiver.

5 qKAI Concept: Utilizing Distributed Web Resources for Enhanced Knowledge Representation

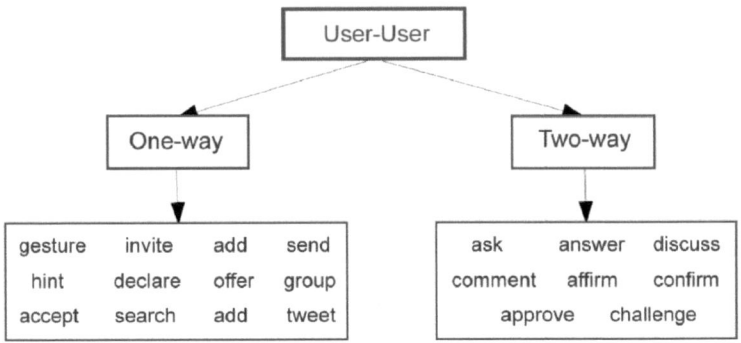

Figure 18: User-User interaction-types [46]

Figure 18 shows the user-user interaction types. Combining the aforementioned criteria results in the social interaction taxonomy illustrated in (**Figure 19**).

qKAI's centerpiece is its interaction rewarding system called GIAR; its architecture is depicted in **Figure 20**. GIAR utilizes game mechanics (see **Chapter 5.2.3**) by mapping them to the (social) interaction taxonomy that has been deduced in this **Chapter 5.2.2**. This mapping leads to a system, which globally rewards (social) interactions independently from the web applications in which they happen. GIAR specifically applies to the following game mechanics, which will be described in more detail in the following chapters [46].

5.2.3 Applied Game Mechanics

In qKAI we currently apply the following game mechanics via GIAR [46]:

- **Points**: Every interaction is rewarded a point value and based on these points, different level types are derived.
- **Collecting**: Users may win and collect interaction rewards that are directly applied to single interactions or general awards applied to interaction-types and classes.

- **Feedback**: GIAR provides feedback about a user's different interaction stats like level states, interaction class and type distribution, rewards earned and user rankings.

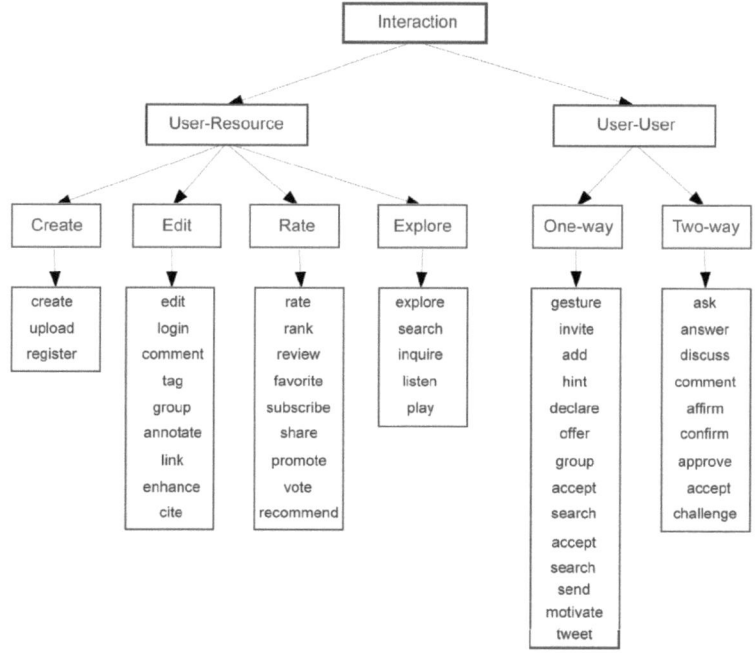

Figure 19: (Social) interaction taxonomy [46]

5.2.4 GIAR Components

The main components of GIAR are depicted in **Figure 20**. This section only points out their main characteristics because further analysis would go beyond the scope of this thesis. Nevertheless, some components will be outlined in more detail in the following sections because they constitute key concepts within GIAR. The ones we will be looking at are the GIAR Config component and the GIAR Config file, which are discussed in more detail in **Chapter 6.5.1**.

5 qKAI Concept: Utilizing Distributed Web Resources for Enhanced Knowledge Representation

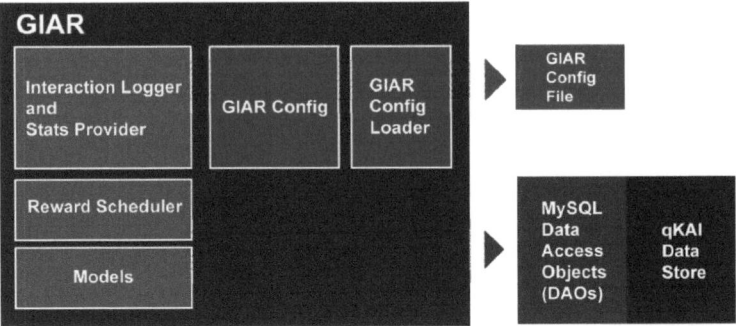

Figure 20: GIAR architecture and used components (based on [46])

Interaction Logger and Stats Provider

This component is used by the RESTful web service methods in Squirl and is comprised of two subcomponents as its name implies. The interaction logger logs interactions, which returns statistics about the logged interaction and how it affects the level states of a user. The stats provider is responsible for aggregating several statistics about users or their interactions. For example, it calculates stats about a user's current level progression or activity distribution and it computes different types of leaderboards. The main task of both components is to acquire and preprocess requested statistics and to create XML or JSON representations that will be returned by RESTful web service methods.

Reward Scheduler

As mentioned before, users may win rewards and qKAI currently offers two types of rewards: rewards for single interactions (e.g. for 100 tagging interactions), and rewards based on aggregated interactions (e.g. for 500 user-user interaction points). Single interaction rewards will be given out at the same moment the interaction is logged. Rewards for aggregated interactions will be given out automatically on a regular basis by the reward scheduler, who uses Quartz [109],, the open source enterprise job scheduler, to schedule the rewarding task. The functional principle of the reward scheduler and which awards it gives out will be presented in **Chapter 5.2.6**.

5.2.5 Points, Levels and Skills

Points

As a basic rewarding mechanism, GIAR assigns a point value between 5 and 100 to each interaction listed in **Figure 20**. According to the reward types presented in **Chapter 3.2.2**, points have a motivational effect on users. They also constitute a basic game mechanic as presented in **Chapter 3.2.1**. The assignment of a point value to an interaction is based on the effort it takes to execute them and corresponds to personal estimation. **Table 5** lists all interactions, which are grouped by interaction-type according to the (social) interaction taxonomy presented in **Figure 17** and their assigned point value.

Interaction type	Interactions and assigned points values
Create	create [100], upload [70], register [50]
Edit	edit [70], login [20], comment [30], tag [20], group [60], annotate [60], link [50], enhance [70], cite [50]
Rate	rate [20], rank [20], review [50], favorite [10], subscribe [10], share [10], promote [10], vote [10], recommend [10]
Explore	inquire [20], explore [20], search [10], listen [5], play [20]
One-way	gesture [10], invite [10], add [5], send [5], hint [10], declare [5], offer [10], group [5], accept [5], search [5], motivate [20], tweet [10], shout [10]
Two-way	ask [30], answer [30], discuss [20], comment [30], affirm [10], confirm [10], approve [10], challenge [10]

Table 5: Points assigned to interactions [46]

Levels and Skills

Level type	Aggregated interactions
global-level	Aggregates *all interactions* from a user and computes a global level value that reveals how active a user is in general
class-level	Aggregates interactions from the two interaction-classes *user-resource* and *user-user* to compute a user-resource-class and a user-user-class level value
skill-level	Aggregates interactions from the interaction-types *create, edit, rate, explore, one-way* and *two-way* and computes a respective level value

Table 6: Level types and aggregated interactions [46]

Based on interaction points, different types of levels and skills have been deduced that map a user's progression. Skills within GIAR have a different meaning than those skill rewards presented in **Chapter 3.2.2** because users do not earn extra skill points that they can freely distribute. A skill within GIAR is a special level type that maps user interactions from the interaction-types, create, edit, rate, explore, one-way and two-way, to a level value. Those level values allow you to make more precise statements about user behavior in web applications, e.g. if a user has a high create skill-level but a low two-way skill-level, it means that she is (relatively) creative and less social and therefore has more creative than social skills. [46]

GIAR-specific implements currently use three level types and all three aggregate different sets of interactions to compute a level value. The level types and their respective aggregated interactions are illustrated in **Table 5**. **Figure 21** depicts this aggregation according to the (social) interaction taxonomy.

There are various options to compute a level value based on aggregated interaction points and game designers spend a lot of effort on creating good level systems, so it is no surprise that most game designers keep their level system a secret, particularly because they do not want the players to game the system. Nevertheless, many

5 qKAI Concept: Utilizing Distributed Web Resources for Enhanced Knowledge Representation

people are interested in how a game computes level values, especially for those games they play regularly. These users in turn spend a lot of time finding out how a game's level system calculation works. During our research, we found a thread in an online forum belonging to the online game Voyage Century [110] that explains how experience points, also referred to as EXP or XP, are mapped to a level value and this calculation is being used within GIAR to calculate user level values. [46]

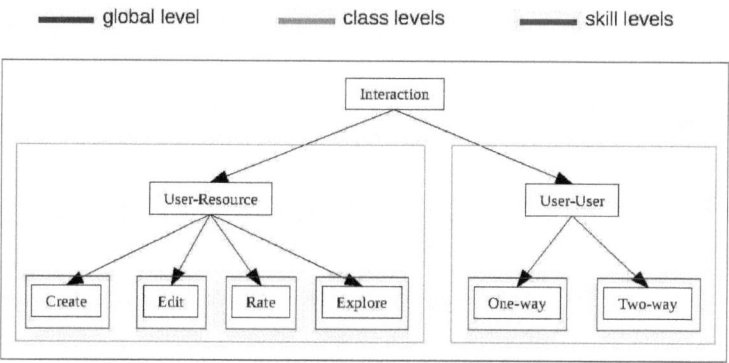

Figure 21: GIAR levels and skills [46]

A level value in GIAR is computed based on the following recursive formula [110] that calculates how many points one needs to reach level x:

$$f(x) = 3 \cdot (const_1 + f(x-1) - f(x-2)) + f(x-3)$$

As this is a recursive formula, further initialization constants other than constant const1 are needed, in particular how many points one needs for the first, second and third levels. [46]

Listing 3 shows the implementation of the given formula with its respective constants (or rather parameters) const1, level1, level2 and level3. The level constants need to meet certain requirements to guarantee correct functioning of the level formula, i.e. the number of points needed for a level increase according to its height. If they do not meet these requirements, it may result in strange results like a negative point value or the number of points needed for a given level may be less than the points needed for a lower level.

```
public int getPointsNeededForLevel(int level){

    switch (level) {
        case 0:
            return 0;
        case 1:
            return level1;
        case 2:
            return level2;
        case 3:
            return level3;
        default:
            return 3 * (const_1 +
                        getPointsNeededForLevel(level - 1) -
                        getPointsNeededForLevel(level - 2)) +
                        getPointsNeededForLevel(level - 3);
    }
}
```

Listing 3: Method to compute points needed for a given level [46]

Constraints to Level Formula Constants:

The following figures outline the effects of varying constant values on points needed for increasing level values.

$$level1 \leq level2 \leq level3$$

$$(level2 - level1) \leq (level3 - level2)$$

$$const_1 > 0$$

5 qKAI Concept: Utilizing Distributed Web Resources for Enhanced Knowledge Representation

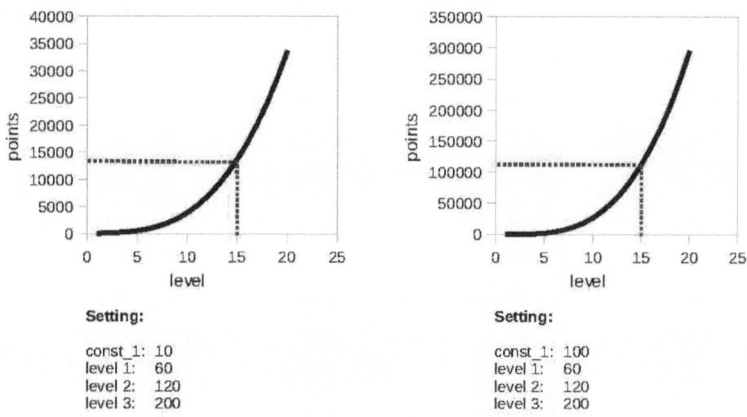

Figure 22: Level constants - example 1 [46]

In example 1 (**Figure 22**), the value of $const_1$ has been increased by a factor of 10 in the right setting; the values of the other constants are equal. In order to reach level 15, a user needs 111,920 points in the right setting, whereas in the left setting only 13,640 points are required, which is about 87% less than in the other setting.

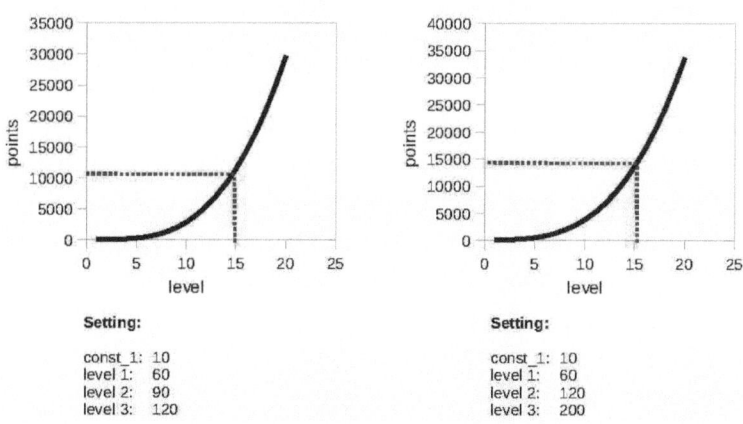

Figure 23: Level constants - example 2 [46]

In example 2 (**Figure 23**), the effect of using different distances between the values of level1, level2 and level3 are shown, whereas

5 qKAI Concept: Utilizing Distributed Web Resources for Enhanced Knowledge Representation

the value of $const_1$ stays the same. The left setting uses equidistant gaps; the right setting uses increasing gaps between the level values. Now, to reach level 15, 11,400 points are needed in the left setting and 13,640 in the right setting, which makes a difference of about 20%. [46]

In summary, it can be stated that the optimal configuration of the level constants depends on various factors, but mostly on how fast users should be able to level up in an application or game. With respect to Squirl, it needs a longer running evaluation to find the optimal values for the constants as it incorporates several, nested level types and different level configurations may have various effects on motivational aspects with regard to user behavior.

Rewards

Squirl rewards user interactions with two types of awards, medals and badges, and thereby adopts the collecting game mechanic presented in **Chapter 2.2.3** in a basic fashion as users may collect these awards.

Medals

Medals are attached to single interactions meaning that a user wins a medal for a certain interaction if she has executed the corresponding interaction X times. As with sports, users may win bronze, silver or gold medals (see **Figure 24**), all having different, increasing X values. Currently, only selected interactions will be rewarded with medals, basically, those interactions that are most common in current (social) web applications or communities, e.g. tag or ask; bronze, silver, gold.

Figure 24: GIAR medals [46]

As soon as an interaction is logged, either via Squirl's REST API or via its web application, Squirl checks to see if the active user has won a medal for the logged interaction by querying the database to find out how often the user has already executed the given interaction. This returned value is used to check the GIAR Config if the newly logged interaction, together with already logged ones, will be rewarded with a medal. [46]

Badges

Badges will be awarded for aggregated user interactions by the Reward Scheduler introduced in **Chapter 5.2.4**. Every Monday at 12:15 a.m., the Reward Scheduler determines those users that have the most activities in an interaction skill or in an interaction class and awards them the following skill and class badges (**Figure 25**):

- Creator of the week: awarded for having most create skill points
- Editor of the week: awarded for having most edit skill points
- Evaluator of the week: awarded for having most rate skill points
- Explorer of the week: awarded for having most explore skill points
- Socializer of the week: awarded for having most user-user interaction class points

Creator Badge Editor Badge Evaluator Badge Explorer Badge Socializer Badge

Figure 25: GIAR skill- and class-badges [46]

Furthermore, on the first of every month (at 12:15 a.m.), the patron of the month badge (**Figure 26**) will be awarded to those users with the most days of activity, weighted by the total number of points of all interactions in the past month. The idea is to reward those users that are regularly active in web applications that use Squirl's rewarding service or within Squirl itself.

Patron Badge

Figure 26: GIAR patron of the month badge [46]

As mentioned before, the Reward Scheduler uses Quartz [109], an open source enterprise job scheduler to schedule the tasks to be awarded. **Listing 4** illustrates the use of Quartz schedulers and jobs to manage the automatic awarding of Squirl badges. [46]

```
1  //Creates and starts schedulers.
2  public void createScheduler() throws SchedulerException, ParseException{
3      SchedulerFactory sf = new StdSchedulerFactory();
4      Scheduler sched = sf.getScheduler();
5      sched.start();
6
7      //scheduled on the first of every month at 0:15
8      JobDetail job1 = new JobDetail("PatronRewarding", sched.DEFAULT_GROUP,
           PatronRewarder.class);
9      CronTrigger triggerMonth = new CronTrigger("monthly", sched.DEFAULT_GROUP, "
           PatronRewarding", sched.DEFAULT_GROUP, "0 15 0 1 * ?");
10     sched.scheduleJob(job1, triggerMonth);
11
12     //scheduled every monday at 0:15
13     JobDetail job2 = new JobDetail("SkillClassRewarding", sched.DEFAULT_GROUP,
           SkillAndClassRewarder.class);
14     CronTrigger triggerWeek = new CronTrigger("weekly", sched.DEFAULT_GROUP, "
           SkillClassRewarding", sched.DEFAULT_GROUP, "0 15 0 ? * MON");
15     sched.scheduleJob(job2, triggerWeek);
16 }
```

Listing 4: Implementation of the reward scheduling method [46]

A scheduler is instantiated by using a SchedulerFactory (**Listing 4, lines 3 and 4**) and must be started before any job is scheduled, otherwise it will not be executed, or rather, their applied triggers will not fire. In **Listing 4, lines 8 and 13**, two jobs are being created and each one of them is responsible for an awarding task. The first job (job1) is responsible for the "Patron of the month" awarding task and will be scheduled at 0:15 on the first of every month. The second job (job2), which will be scheduled every Monday at 0:15, is responsible for the skill and class badge awarding task. Next, two CronTriggers (lines 9 and 14) are being created and they are responsible for the execution of their attached jobs. Their "firing time" is configured by a cron expression (last parameter of the CronTrigger) that describes the scheduling properties. A cron expression is made up of seven sub-expressions as depicted in **Table 7** and they must be specified in the given order (from left to right). **Table 7** shows the cron expressions used to trigger the awarding jobs for the patron, skill and class badges. [46]

| | Cron Expression | | | | | | |
Job	seconds	minutes	hours	day-of-month	month	day-of-week	year (optional)
job1	0	15	0	1	*	?	
job2	0	15	0	?	*	MON	

Table 7: Cron Expressions for awarding jobs [46]

5.2.6 Feedback

Feedback is a crucial element of every system that supports user interactions. However, especially in gamelike systems, feedback is not only used to indicate that an interaction was *successful,* e.g. "you have beaten the boss," or unsuccessful, e.g. "game over." Feedback is also used to help users keep track of their progression, which is the focus of qKAI's feedback-system. qKAI provides different types of feedback as listed below:

- Feedback on single (logged) interactions
- Feedback on user rankings (leaderboards)
- Feedback on general user statistics

The latter two types of feedback can be accessed via Squirl's REST API and via its web application interface (partially), whereas feedback on single logged interactions is only provided via the REST API. The web application also rewards and logs certain user interactions, but feedback is not given directly or immediately. For example, via a pop-up, as it might decrease usability of its user interface. All feedback types and their representations will be illustrated in more detail in **Chapters 6.5, 6.8** and **7.1**.

Feedback on Single Interactions

Every interaction that is logged via qKAI's REST API (compare **Chapter 7.1**) gives feedback on the interaction itself and on its effect on the levels belonging to the interaction. In other words, its effect on a user's global level, as well as on the corresponding class and skill level. With respect to an interaction, feedback is given on the number of points it earns, the interaction type and interaction class to which it belongs, the total number of times the interaction has been executed so far, its name and if a medal has been unlocked. With respect to each level affected, feedback is given on the total number of points, the current level, the number of points needed to reach the next level, the level name and if the user has leveled up.

Feedback on User Rankings

Squirl incorporates several user rankings as leaderboards, all having a different focus on interactions and they are based either on (aggregated) points, or on the number of executed interactions. According to each level type that Squirl implements, a corresponding leader board can be requested: A global leader board that ranks users by their total number of points, interaction-class leaderboards ranking users based on aggregated user-resource or user-user interaction points and finally interaction type leader boards aggregating interaction points in each interaction skill. Based on the number of executed interactions, activity leaderboards can be requested. They rank users according to their activities and with respect to a certain point in time. This means that they aggregate all the activities that happened in the current year, month or week. With respect to the "Patron of the month" badge, a patron leader board can be requested that ranks users by the number of distinct days of being active, weighted by the total number of activities within the respective month.

Feedback on User Statistics

There are various statistics about users and their interactions available within Squirl. Users may request their current ranking within the different leaderboards presented in the previous paragraph or they may request all the awards they have won so far. Other statistics available make statements about a user's activity distribution regarding interaction class and interaction type, current state and progression in the level types presented in **Chapter 5.2.5** (points, levels and skills), and activity progression over a certain period of time (i.e. how active), in terms of executed interactions for a user in the current year, month or week.

5.3 User Activity and Quality of Resources

In the following, we present our adaption of **information quality** (iq) aspects to qualify web resources based on a three-level assessment model. We deploy knowledge-related iq-criteria as a tool to implement iq-mechanisms into the qKAI framework step by step. Here, we show examples of selected criteria determining the quality of information in qKAI, e.g. relevance and accuracy.

We derived assessment methods for iq-criteria, which enable rich, game-based user interaction and semantic resource annotation. Open Content is embedded into knowledge games to increase the user access and learning motivation. As a positive side effect, the quality of the resource is gradually enhanced by ongoing user interaction. Using the example of image tag rating in folksonomies, we demonstrate a practicable use case for qualifying web resources by a keyword-oriented group search and game-based tag ranking in detail.

One prerequisite to reusing distributed web resources, especially in knowledge transfer and learning, is that the quality of the content needs to be good. To determine statements about a resource's quality, information about the resource is necessary. **The more we know about the resource, the better we can reuse it.** We cannot say which resource or content is "good", but maybe we can determine which resource is the better one.

5 qKAI Concept: Utilizing Distributed Web Resources for Enhanced Knowledge Representation

Metadata is an important factor in analyzing and categorizing content. In the case of missing metadata, automated and manual annotations are approved workarounds to get information about the information, while deriving useful knowledge from it. Assessing the quality of information quality (e.g. provenance, reputation, timeliness, and correctness) is important for further deployment in knowledge transfer scenarios and can be deduced from the metadata analysis and other interactive assessment criteria. Every kind of activity or interaction between a user and a resource invokes more implicit information about the resource involved (stored as a new annotation of the resource). A simple example annotation is the popularity of a resource because of its overall, system-wide hits (number of requests).

The issue of content quality arises, especially when enabling User Generated Content (UGC) that is not authored by experts, but is still used for knowledge transfer scenarios. Therefore, we developed a three-level model to handle different aspects of quality. Metadata can be seen as a quality feature [103]. The more metadata we snap, the better we get to know the content. There is no absolute quality, but we can compare resources (Open World Assumption) and weigh them based on the amount and structure of meta-information. Enrichment of a resource happens in a corresponding qKAI URI by semantic interlinking. One example is a domain ranking visualized as tag clouds to show which domain we get the most information from in real time. First level criteria contain metadata directly included in a resource, like format, timeliness, author, provenance or language, which can be automatically detected. Second level criteria are determined through user interaction, which helps to enhance semantic correctness. Regarding factual knowledge like "Berlin lies at the Spree" or "Hanover is the capital of Lower Saxony," we see user rating and ranking according to the established Web 2.0 manner as an effective solution to marking wrong content and ranking valuable or popular content systematically. Alongside this crowd sourcing community approach, role and level-based quality control mechanisms are also possible.

Content that is delivered gradually can be qualified this way. Resources are marked according to their quality level as either reviewed, proofed or not yet qualified, to enable embedding on different levels of knowledge transfer and learning. Third level criteria are inferred by employing Natural Language Processing to detect additional information hidden inside a resource.

5.3.1 Quality of Content

In qKAI information quality (iq) is deployed as a tool to derive quality metrics and to determine measurable quality criteria.

Iq-Criteria for the qKAI System Domain

It is not practicable to measure all available iq-criteria at once. We have to select the most important criteria for our domain. In qKAI, the focus is on knowledge transfer with smart interaction. To offer knowledge-related content, we have to fulfill semantically correctness of factual data. We interpret semantic correctness as one aspect of accuracy. Accuracy is defined as the degree of correctness and precision with which information in an information system represents states of the real world [107]. **Figure 27** shows the current most important iq-criteria in the qKAI system domain.

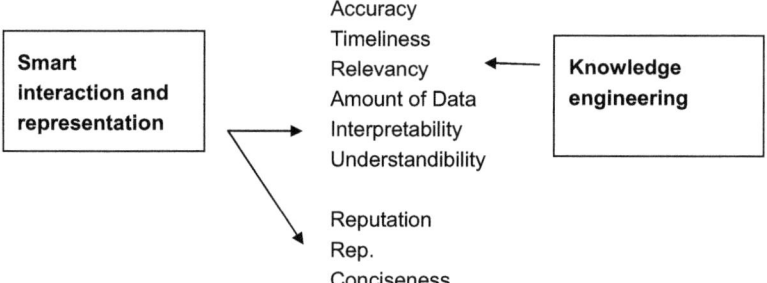

Figure 27: Most relevant iq-criteria for the qKAI system domain: knowledge transfer and smart interaction based on autonomous resources.

Technical criteria (also called accessibility criteria) like availability, response time or security mostly depend on soft and hardware. We developed the qKAI hybrid data layer as part of the qKAI mashup framework to provide good results for the technical criteria on an affordable Quadcore platform. qKAI is suitable for searching and exploring distributed resources in an effective manner and represents our ongoing and enhanced research in hybrid data management for distributed resources layered with rich interaction. To reach good results in the frontend, the backend, including the data layer, has to be suitable for this purpose. E.g., if a user waits too long to get the first search results, his motivation to continue the interaction will rapidly decrease. The iq-criteria "response time" and "availability" have to be enhanced by technical aspects like hard or software requirements.

Reputation as a Criteria of Quality and User Motivation

Reputation can be seen as the sum of single experiences and expectations about the trustworthiness and competence of a person, a group or an organization. Reputation has much to do with the image and status of a person or thing and is an important factor in online communities, where trust and reliability come into play. Most online communities that collect feedback to qualify content do not offer any rating and ranking incentives. Users' lack of motivation with regard to interacting with the content is an essential problem. They do not see why they should continue participating if the chance to participate in the rating process is taken from them [111]. Creating and enhancing their own reputation is next to the simple fun [49] a good motivator to embed online users into to content-related participation without material incentive [111] [103]. Ebay and Amazon are successful examples for building reputation with user feedback. In qKAI, the reputation of users is stored implicitly in their personal profile and increases with every interaction on Open Content. A resource reputation is stored in their semantically linked qKAI annotated URI, and is increased by any interaction or analysis that involves the resource.

5.3.2 A Three-Level Qualifying Model

"Information quality assessment is the process of assigning numerical values (iq-scores) to iq-criteria. An iq-score reflects one aspect of information quality of a set of data items." [100]

To assess the iq of information sources, a scoring function calculates assessment scores from the collected ratings. The scoring function decides which ratings are taken into account, and might assign different weights to the ratings. The user should be able to adapt the criteria for a specific rating or purpose. In general, our research showed that the following classifications and assessment models are the most suitable for web-based information systems with knowledge-related concerns. Naumann [100] identified three main factors, which influence the quality of information in his query-oriented approach:

- The perception of the user (the subject of a query)

- The data itself (the object of a query)
- The process of accessing the data (the predicate of a query)

C. Bizer [103] derived three levels of information quality metrics in web-based information systems:

- **Content-Based Metrics** use the information to be assessed as a quality indicator in itself. The information itself is analyzed or compared with related information.
- **Context-Based Metrics** employ meta-information for the information content and the circumstances in which the information was created, e.g. who said what and when, as quality indicator.
- **Rating-Based Metrics** rely on explicit ratings about the information itself, information sources, or information providers. Ratings may originate from the information consumer, other information consumers, or domain experts.

We adjusted the three levels to assess iq for qKAI needs to the first, second and third level assessment and divided them into the following categories: **metadata analysis**, **user interaction** and **intelligent analysis**.

There is no absolute quality, but we can compare resources (Open World Assumption) and weigh them based on the amount and structure of metadata. Enrichment of a resource happens in a corresponding qKAI URI by semantic interlinking and annotation. Ranking according to available metadata properties or interaction history is possible too.

The qKAI concept here provides assessment and enhancement of the content's information quality criteria according to game-based user interaction. This kind of content evaluation and annotation can be regarded as one more task in knowledge engineering that is solvable by gaming mechanics.

First Level Assessment: Metadata Analysis

According to Bizer [103], this level enables **context-based assessment** of metadata directly related to a resource like format, timeliness, author, provenance or language, which can be automatically detected. Metadata can be seen as a quality feature.

The more metadata we extract, the better we get to know the content. In qKAI, we implement the support of Aperture [35] to fetch Dublin core elements [112] such as the ones listed in **Table 8**.

Element	Definition and recommended value formats
Title	A name given to a resource Value format: Free text
Creator	The entity primarily responsible for creating the resource content Value format: Name as free text
Subject	The topic of the resource Value formats: Library of Congress Subject Headings (LCSH), Medical Subject Headings (MeSH), Dewy Decimal Classification (DDC)
Description	An account of the resource content Value format: Free text
Publisher	The entity responsible for making the resource available Value format: Name as free text
Contributor	The entity responsible for making contributions to the content of the resource Value format: Name as free text
Date	The date the resource was created or made available Value Format: W3C-DTF
Type	The nature or genre of the content of the resource Value Format: DCMI Type Vocabulary
Format	The physical or digital manifestation of the resource Value Format: MIME-Type
...	...

Table 8: Exemplary Dublin Core element set for metadata [112]

Comparable iq scores can be derived from adjustable quality policies like available metadata property count: The less metadata properties a resource contains, the smaller is its iq score is for believability or reputation. Even provenance and timeliness are very important aspects concerning trust with regard to the content of a resource. Information about the author is also very relevant for the quality of the resource. A user with high personal scores in certain knowledge domains has a high reputation in this area. We can speak of local reputation here, because it is dependent in the same way the iq-criteria are — from task to user and context.

Second Level Assessment: User Interaction

Here, we allocate criteria that can be assessed with the help of user interaction. Questionnaires are often used to get user feedback for this purpose. According to Bizer, this is called **rating-based assessment.**

The user can help enhance accuracy, even with regard to semantic correctness. To evaluate factual knowledge like "Berlin lies at the Spree" or "Hanover is the capital of Lower Saxony," we see user rating and ranking according to the established Web 2.0 manner as an effective solution for marking wrong content and ranking valuable or popular content step by step. Alongside this crowd sourcing community approach, we present role and level-based quality control mechanisms. Lecturers earn rewards while rating and creating educational resources in Open Content; students earn rewards while answering questions, managing gaming tasks, exploring further content or ranking their favorites. Content presented in steps can be qualified this way.

Integrating online assessment components like multiple-choice or assignment question types into socially oriented software seems to be a new approach. Although online assessment and rating mechanisms have many things in common and can be complementary, a combination of the two has not yet been introduced.

Third Level Assessment: Intelligent Analysis

Content-based assessment employs Natural Language Processing to detect additional information hidden inside a resource. Aperture [35] and Virtuoso Spongers [36], for example, enable comprehensive solutions for these tasks. f more text engineering is needed, there are comprehensive solutions for standard Natural Language Processing (NLP) tasks (e.g. by OpenNLP [37]) to perform sentence detection, Named Entity Recognition (NER), Part-Of-Speech (POS) tagging or even semantic chunking. **Table 9** shows the related iq-criteria, their categories and whether their assessment is subjective or objective.

Category	Criteria/ Dimension	Objective/ Subjective
Intrinsic criteria (Independent of the user's context)	Accuracy*	Objective
	Consistency	Objective
	Objectivity	Objective
	Timeliness	Objective
Contextual criteria (Context, task and user dependent)	Believability	Subjective
	Completeness	Subjective
	Understandability	Subjective
	Relevancy	Subjective
	Reputation	Subjective
	Verifiability	Subjective
	Amount of Data	Subjective
Representational criteria (Spell out Rep.)	Interpretability	Subjective
	Rep. Conciseness	Subjective
	Rep. Consistency	Objective
Accessibility criteria	Availability	Objective
	Response Time	Objective
	Security	Objective

Table 9: Interaction tasks, assigned rewarding points and improvable iq-criteria

When we talk about information quality, we are also talking about user preferences and personalization. It is obvious that many of the iq-criteria are relevant while user interaction takes place, because they are subjective – user, task and context dependent. Most of the iq-criteria have a direct impact on the user's interaction. There are only a few iq-criteria like "amount of data" or "completeness," that can be assessed with little or no user interaction at all. Even technical criteria influences usability, ease of use and user motivation. Without fulfilling technical criteria in a sufficient way, smart interaction is not possible on the user side. Altogether, the second level of our qualifying model with strong focus on user interaction is the most important and influential one if we want to determine relevant, but subjective iq scores.

5.3.3 Quality Assessment with the Help of User Interaction

Incentive for user participation is implemented as a global rewarding system of any interaction in qKAI (GIAR, Squirl). **Table 10** shows interaction types, their assigned reward in the form of gaming points and improvable iq-criteria. Every interaction is based on a resource, and implements different types of interactions.

Interaction	Reward	Improvable iq-criteria
Edit	+50 points	Accuracy, consistency, objectivity, timeliness, believability, reputation, completeness, understandability
Create	+100 points	Completeness, accuracy, verifiability, amount of data
Annotate/add/interlink	+50 points	Completeness, accuracy, verifiability, amount of data, interpretability, understandability
Rate/rank	+10 points	Relevancy, accuracy, believability, reputation, objectivity, interpretability, understandability, rep. conciseness

Table 10: Interaction tasks, assigned rewarding points and improvable iq-criteria

Here the connection between information quality assessment and GIAR is obvious: the global interaction rewarding mechanism (described in detail in **Chapter 5.2**) interacts with the quality of the content and information respectively. This is an important aspect because one of the main concepts of qKAI is to enhance the content's quality by the user's interaction while keeping the user motivated in continuing interoperation with other resources.

Simple and Direct Feedback

Like in common surveys and evaluation, rating is done with questionnaires with predefined scores. These ratings can evaluate persons, resources or knowledge units.

Enhanced Feedback and Game-Based Interaction

Every resource that is visualized or just queried by qKAI can be rated and ranked by user interaction or automated metrics like metadata detection. The more a resource is requested, the more statistical data we gain. The more we know about a resource, the better we can personalize its usage.

Next to editing, creating, annotating, adding, interlinking and rating resources and users, we offer the following game-based options.

qRANK (see **Chapter 7.3**) is an example where the user rates and ranks by using tags while playing a drag and drop browser game with Flickr [6] images.

Indirect and Automated Feedback

History protocols and interaction recording allows statistics to be deduced for rating and ranking purposes. Therefore, Simple Scoring Functions, Collaborative Filtering, Web-of-Trust Algorithms or Flow Models can be deployed in the future

5.3.4 Quality of Interaction

During this thesis, the quality of interaction is defined as usability in combination with social aspects (quality of interaction = usability + social aspects). Beyond standard usability issues, we want to consider criteria like motivation to participate, ongoing attendance and incentive. If we find a way of classifying an interaction task at first glance, we are able to deduce more quality aspects analyzing a user's interaction results with other users and resources.

Steve Krug gets to the heart of the matter in his book, *Don't Make Me Think!* He says that people want to use the Web without thinking too much about how to do it. We also speak of "intuitive" usage in the context of Human-Computer Interaction (HCI) and interface design.

If a user has **fun while interacting**, this can be interpreted as a **high quality of interaction**. Incentive enhances the quality of interaction.

There is a connection between game design elements and user interaction quality, but what is the connection between **quality** and **user interaction**? It has to do with the principles of common usability, as well as how well an interoperation deals with a task.

Some of the aspects that should be fulfilled by focusing on user interaction quality are:

- Easy to use, intuitive
- Adjustable functional range, scope of operation, personalization
- Flexible and not boring
- Adaptive
- Attractive, well organized, clearly arranged
- Smooth and graceful dialog
- Meaningful feedback

- Enhanced, non-boring interaction tasks ("exciting" interaction).

Overall, quality of interaction in qKAI is defined as the interplay of usability and social aspects, with the aim to satisfy the user's expectation as good and interesting as possible. The term "user experience" is currently popular and describes the desirable state of user interaction in web applications (see **Chapter 2.4.4**).

5.3.5   Tag Quality and Ranking in Folksonomies

We derived **keyword-oriented group search and ranking mechanisms** to find relevant pictures in folksonomies like Flickr. [124]

Groups in communities allow pre-selected content and increase the precision and relevance of the recall. Our idea to improve search results is a keyword-oriented group search and ranking. We developed a tag ranking game called qRANK to rate and rank web resources. Flickr allows its users to organize pictures in groups and related groups in collections. Groups, tags, views and comments contain important information that could help us learn about folksonomies. The aim of this work is not to develop a global algorithm for the complex search problem in folksonomies.

Rather, we implemented and evaluated ideas and methods to optimize photo relevance and quality for web photo searches [124]. A methodology, which allows an automatic classification and ranking of photos based on their attractiveness was developed [113]. Photo attractiveness is a very subjective term that depends on many factors. The feedback from the user will supply important information for classification and regression models to be created, based on the visual characteristics of the images and metadata.

"In a wider system context, such techniques can be useful to enhance ranking functions for photo search, and, more generally, to complement mining and retrieval methods based on text, other metadata and social dimensions." [113]

5 qKAI Concept: Utilizing Distributed Web Resources for Enhanced Knowledge Representation

Visual features such as color, contrast and rudeness of images and other metadata such as tags and favorites lists are examined. The combination of visual and textual features yielded the best results for the ranking according to a photo's attractiveness.

Figure 28: Flickr standard search for the terms „Rathaus" and „Hannover".

Here the main issue is the quality of the image search. The quality of a search result is determined by the intention of the searcher. Therefore, it is worthwhile to study the search behavior and motivation of a user carefully. In general, a user has the following interests:

- **Precise search:** The user is looking for a specific image or images, such as the Eiffel Tower.
- **Search topics:** The user is looking for a picture or pictures on a specific topic, such as black cats or a particular breed of dog.
- **He has no particular intention** of searching, but is curios and wants a closer look at village (vicinity search).

Attractiveness of Pictures

This approach should help determine the precision of the images by the attractiveness and popularity of the photos. A scenario for an exact search might look like this: A user searches for a picture of the new city hall in Hanover to use for a presentation he has to give at school. He used the two keywords "Rathaus" and "Hannover." Therefore, the standard keyword-search in Flickr provides 175 results. We can display the first ten images at random and get the following pictures as seen in **Figure 28**. There are also some images of the town hall however, none of this is what he really wants to use for his work. Still, of the 175 photos, there are some that correspond to what he has in mind; however, the user wants to find the photo that is relevant to his search as soon as possible. The relevance of the image here refers to the given information content of the user, since, generally speaking, all images may be relevant. The intent of the user (presentation for class) implies that the content of the image must clearly satisfy the search term. Relevance is indeed a relationship between an image and a user. A tag and a picture are defined as relevant, if the tag only describes aspects of the visual content of an image [114] [124].

In the course of this work, we call relevance (also used in precision) the degree to which the content of an image corresponds to the search criteria entered. This degree of precision can be used to classify images. Apart from the problem that many images cannot be found because they were not annotated with enough tags or the tags were inaccurate, there is the problem of assessing the degree of relevance. For some queries, you get a very large selection of Flickr images that are differ in their relevance. Since one is usually interested in just a few of these images, a ranking of the images returned by the search is required. There is a patented publication of Yahoo! for Flickr, which deals with this problem [115]. There are five criteria for ranking by interestingness in narrow folksonomies:

1. The number of tags to a document
2. The number of people tagging a document
3. The number of users that receive the document after the search

4. The relevance of the tags
5. The time frame (the older the document, the less relevant it is)

Most of these criteria are closely related. The first two criteria are important for the relevance of the tags. If multiple users annotate an image with different terms, they create a multidimensional view of the resource. Suitably chosen tags facilitate the search. If the terms are very different, the search is inaccurate. An image that was tagged by different users also reflects the popularity of this picture. Photos, which are described with many tags, are found more often. The criterion of time is not applicable, because a picture does not lose its relevance over time. The feature "interestingness" is described in Flickr by W. Stock and I. Peters [115] as follows:

"Many factors affect whether something is on Flickr interesting (or not). It depends on the origin of the clicks, who commented when the image of who identifies it as a favorite, which tags are used, and many more factors that change constantly."

Since the components are related, this feature is deliberately not discussed in more depth. Derived from [115], we define three different sets of criteria for the ranking in tagged documents (see **Figure 29**), which are of importance for our work.

5 qKAI Concept: Utilizing Distributed Web Resources for Enhanced Knowledge Representation

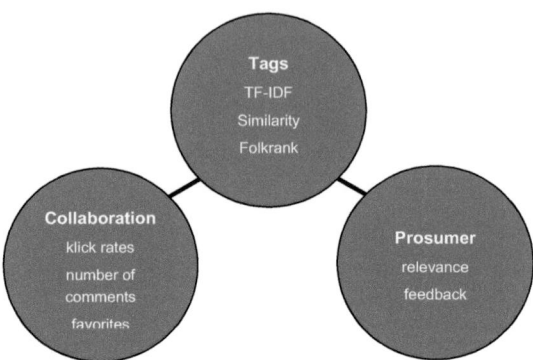

Figure 29: Ranking criteria in folksonomies

The first volume contains procedures that relate to the semantics of the tags. The relevance of the tags can be determined using the method presented in the previous section as the TF-IDF weighting, the cosine similarity or the FolkRank algorithm. In addition to these criteria, there are other factors, such as click-through rates, the number of comments and favorites list, which can be crucial to a relevant search (collaboration). In addition, you can include the relevance of terms, and the feedback of the users with (prosumer). This can be done in a question-answer game, where users assess metadata of resources.

For a relevant search, some of the investigated options shown in **Figure 29** are examined. For the next approach, we use the **click-through rates** and the **upload date** of the pictures and examine whether images, which are often viewed at the same time have a higher relevance. With the interface of the Flickr API, click rates (views) of each picture and the upload date can be fetched. The number of clicks is an implicit relevance feedback, *"they are in a high degree collaboration-oriented ranking criterion in the sense of Web 2.0."* [115].

Mark an image as a favorite reflects the attraction and popularity of the image. In general, one can assume that by increasing the click rate, the number of favorites raises. Therefore, we extended our search with an additional function that sorts the pictures by clicking the spending rate. The click rate is a picture dependent of the upload date. Photos that are online longer generally have a higher click rate than actual pictures. To counteract this, the upload time in the calculation is considered. This function is called the precision formula, which results from the division of the click rate and the time (in seconds) that a picture is already online. In combining the precision of the ranking formula for interestingness, the relevance of the retrieval set is clearly improved.

The same search from the previous example, sorted according to the precision value, returns the data shown in **Figure 30** with the first ten images that the user receives after a search for "Rathaus Hannover." The weakness of this method is that the images are very new, and are assigned a higher weight than older ones. An image that has ten clicks on the first day would have a very high precision value without being necessarily relevant for our search. The click through rate alone is not an absolute indicator of the relevance of a search. The click-through rate of an image rather reflects their popularity. This in turn depends on several factors. As a rule, Flickr photos that belong to a broad community are looked at often. Images that contain many groups, and its creators, are linked with many other users that generally have higher click rates. This means that the pictures are not relevant for a subject search but may be very popular. In the section "Flickr groups" of this chapter, an approach is presented on how images grow in relevance. [124]

Figure 30: Extended Flickr search for the terms „Rathaus Hannover" with precision formula

A major problem in the search for relevant images is the ambiguity of the tags. The tag "Paris" can mean a city in France or a city in the U.S. or even refer to a name. When the user searches the tag "Paris" for pictures of the French capital, he will receive, among other things pictures from America or from people who are called Paris. This could be reduced if we refine the query with related terms. In the research on folksonomies, this approach is called the "tag of suggestion" [116] or tag recommendation approach [117] [118] and can be used for two things. First, you can use it to help the users support the annotation. Recommendations will help users clarify the image content as well as reminding them of related semantics, which may otherwise be ignored [117]. On the other hand, we can extend the inquiry with other tags in order to achieve a more relevant search. We will concentrate here on the second approach.

Tag Suggestion

The idea of tag suggestion is used in this section to specify the search for images. From previous considerations, we know that tags are ambiguous, imprecise and often irrelevant. Linguistic differences and the fact that users are not professional taggers, makes it difficult to find the pictures in Flickr. If a user has annotated a picture with the words "cat," "white," and "charly," we will not find this picture if we search for the keyword "Katze" (German translation). In Flickr, there are twice as many images that are tagged as "cat" rather than "Katze," and as many pictures that are tagged as "cats" instead of "cat." Even if these images actually reflect the same content, they form different result sets in Flickr. A work about tag list in folksonomies combines an image with relevant concepts from other sources, such as WordNet [114].

This thesis focuses primarily on the query and tries to **isolate the problem of imprecise tagging**, as we show related tags to the user automatically. Here the question is expanded by the user with the selected terms. Based on the above example, the user gets a list of related tags containing terms like "cat" and "cats" while searching for "Katze." These are terms that occur together often with the search word (co-occurrence relationships). By extending the search to several terms, the number of results also increases.

The query extension can be used to narrow the search further. This is used in qMAP (compare **Chapter 7.2.1**) to reduce the problem of synonyms. If a user searches for the word "apple", it is not clear whether this term refers to the fruit "apple" or to the company "Apple." Such an inquiry would yield many irrelevant images. However, if the request is extended with an additional term such as "fruit" or "Mac," then its ambiguity is eliminated. In this simple case, the searcher possibly finds out on his own that his request is not clear and would change or expand his search with a different term. In most cases, however, a user does not worry about whether his chosen search term is ambiguous and much less tries to find an appropriate term with which he can formulate his question precisely. An improperly selected tag means that the results are again irrelevant or relevant images are not found.

A selection of tags that are related to the term used by the user in a strong correlation facilitates the search. In qMAP the user gets a list of related tags available for the selection in the query extension. The terms selected by the user are involved in the request and only images are displayed that contain the tag list and all of the keywords. A multi-query search is also suitable for general subject searches: A user searches for a specific topic such as black cats. This is the request for "cat" extended with the term "black" and searched for images that contain both words. In response, the user gets only pictures that contain one of the two concepts "cat" and "black." For a more precise topic search, this version is less suitable. Knowing that many images are annotated inaccurately, it can be assumed that the method of query expansion also provides images that do not contain any black cats. On the other hand, there are also pictures that would have been useful to the user on the context, but are not found due to the lack of tags. The number of tags per image is very limited in Flickr [6]. This is because most of the pictures are annotated only by the creator and are not tagged with many words. In addition, a user does not take the time to worry about and discuss alternative and more detailed tags. In contrast, the groups at Flickr are used more often. A study in [119] has found out that over half of the users (about 8 million) share at least one Flickr photo with a group. Flickr groups are self-organized communities with common interests [119]. A closer look at Flickr groups would be an important step in find relevant images that were either inaccurately tagged or not tagged at all. In this study, the groups are used primarily for subject searches.

Flickr Groups

A group is a collection of people and objects that either are in physical proximity or share certain abstract properties. The main goal of a group is to facilitate the exchange of resources in a community. In contrast to the similarity graph in previous sections, groups are not generated algorithmically. They arise spontaneously, not by chance:

"Users participate in groups by sharing and commenting on photos, most often on specific topics or themes, like a popular event, location, or photographic style." [119]

Such collective behavior modes offer alternative ways in understanding and analyzing visual content. Grouping is a simple and well-received folksonomy function, which provides valuable information to detect relevant resources and improves the quality of the search [120]. Most groups had a clear theme, and are sorted in this context issues.

"Two images are similar if they belong to the same Flickr group." [121]

Users who are involved usually have the same interests. They exchange information and knowledge through group discussions and comments about the pictures. The resulting collective intelligence enables better annotation of the pictures in well-moderated groups. Members, who are friends with each other, develop similar approaches to an image. In [108] the grouping effect in a tagging system is presented with Group Me! in which the user can organize any of the resources from other tagging systems in groups via drag and drop. Group Me! allows not only tagging of resources, but also tagging of the groups themselves. The annotation of resources can always be considered within the context of a particular group. This provides additional relationships that can be used for the quality of the resource ranking:

"Tagging resources is always done in context of a certain group. This group context gains new relations between entities of the GroupMe! folksonomy, which consists of user-tag-resource-group bindings, e.g. the group's tags are likely to be relevant for the mem-

bers of the group, and vice versa. Such new relations enable advanced folksonomy-based ranking strategy." [122].

A ranking algorithm is presented in Group Me! that uses the effect of the grouping for the ranking in folksonomies. The "gRank" algorithm based on FolkRank returns through use of the group structure has better results than the general FolkRank algorithm [123].

In Flickr groups there are collections of people who voluntarily join a community. The collections of resources that are collected by the group members are called a "group pool". Each user can create any number of groups. Three different types of groups are crucial to these searches:

- Public, everyone can see the group photos and join the group.
- Public, everyone can see the pictures and membership is by invitation only.
- Private, no one can find the group and membership is by invitation only.

Here, we concentrate on public groups only. In [119], the group structure of Flickr is analyzed. The average number of members per group is approximately 317 (**Figure 31**).

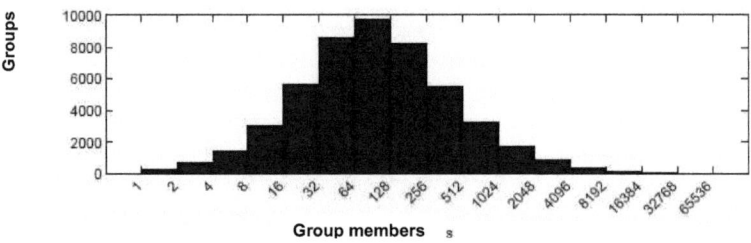

Figure 31: Analysis of Flickr groups "number of members" [119]

5 qKAI Concept: Utilizing Distributed Web Resources for Enhanced Knowledge Representation

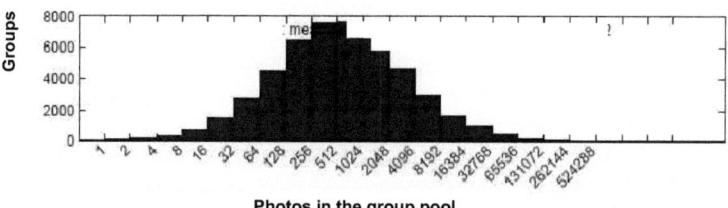

Figure 32: Analysis of Flickr groups "total images" [119]

Unfortunately, there are also many groups in Flickr with very few members or even groups without images. These provide no information and are known as "spam groups." The average number of photos in a group is approximately 3,191 photos (**Figure 32**).

Both images are a proof that the exchange of photos in groups is an important activity among Flickr users. More than 50% of the users share at least one picture with a group. Over 25% of the members share at least 50 images [119]. A photo can also be included in several groups. Groups ensure a higher exposure of the photos. They offer the user a wide selection of relevant images for a specific topic and make the photos easier to find. Just as difficult as the search for images, is the search for relevant groups:

"*In practice, finding groups on Flickr is relatively cumbersome and does not make use of the plethora of meta-data available in the user groups and photo collections.*"[119].

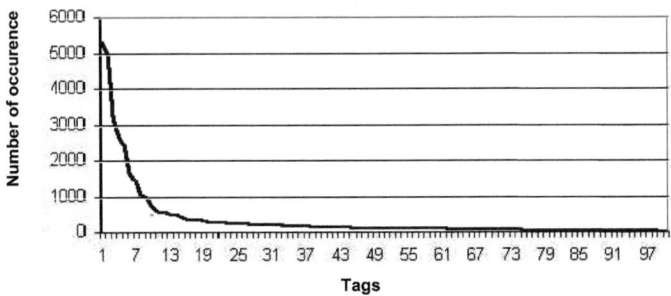

Figure 33: Example tag distribution in a Flickr group

Groups are found in Flickr first through their group name or description. The title of a group is not always perfect. The description is often too broad irrelevant and there are too many groups for a specific topic. According to [119], 60% of the groups consist of one to five relevant subjects and only in 10% of the groups, do we find more than ten subjects. Unlike in Group Me!, users can only annotate the pictures in Flickr. The number of tags in a group is therefore limited by the maximum of 75 words that can be used to describe the images. **Figure 33** shows the 100 most used tags in a group with a total of 15,222 elements. At the beginning of the curve, a few tags are placed that have high values, and the right end is composed of many nearly equivalent tags. This type of distribution, which is similar to a **power law curve** (compare **Figure 34**), was discovered in broad folksonomies by T. Vander Wal. [115]

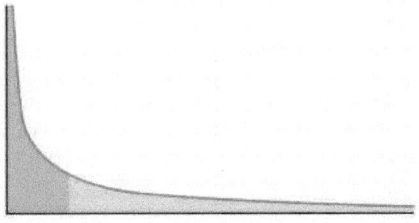

Figure 34: Power-Law curve [115]

The tag distribution of the Flickr groups is almost identical to the ideal power law function. The green area in **Figure 34** contains tags that are found in most resources. These reflect the collective opinion of the group members and are more relevant for a group's subject. In the yellow area, we find the "Long Tail" including special tags. These are subjective tags that are not as related to the subject of the group. There are no annotated Flickr groups, so one can derive the tags of the images to the groups when considering the groups as one resource. The tags, which occur frequently, are more relevant to the topic in the group. For detailed information about our group mechanics, please see [124].

From the previous considerations, we now deduce our tag-based search and ranking procedure for Flickr groups. The approach builds on the search methods used in Flickr, but then considers ranking of the search results by the most used tags in each group. In addition, this method eliminates groups that have little or no elements. For the ranking of the groups following is information that should be considered:

- The members and the number of elements
- The most used tags with a weighting factor
- The titles and the descriptions of the groups

The idea is that groups that contain most of the pictures in the ratio for the given tag are most relevant for a subject search. Since the groups are primarily used to get the most images for a specific subject, only those groups are interesting that provide a certain number of images. Therefore, the group ranking process ranks the groups according to the quantity of images that are annotated with the desired keyword. The most commonly used tags are elected as representatives of the groups.

5.4 Related Work

Wang [106], Naumann [100] and Bizer [103] et al. have done considerable research on categorization, the definition of information quality and related terms in the domain of a web-based information system. Wikipedia [4] has its own quality assessment deploying a review mode by authors. Freebase [15] allows the user to rearrange, connect, correct or annotate available resources. Rating, ranking and recommendation at Amazon [55] are good examples of enhanced user interaction to qualify content. Flickr offers properties related to a picture that enable a user to rate a photo's quality. Tagging allows users to restructure and weigh their knowledge in a user-controlled way. Revyu [107] allows the users to rank and rate everything. In qKAI we will integrate Revyu by querying whether a resource has been annotated by Revyu. The reputation of a thing, person or resource in qKAI is increased if there is a Revyu entry about it. The existence of available interlinked context information in other web platforms, for example, is a first and simple step in determining the quality of information of resources by using scores.

5.5 Summary

The qKAI concept builds the conceptual basis and background for the qKAI mashup framework described in **Chapter 6** and the relying application scenarios described in **Chapter 7**.

qKAI focuses on three main aspects while utilizing distributed resources that are exemplary for enhanced knowledge representation:

1. Open Content builds a distributed and interlinked knowledge base for different kinds of interactive knowledge systems.
2. A global interaction rewarding (GIAR) model based on a global, interaction taxonomy integrates basic gaming principles into web applications in a generic and global way as a meta-rewarding system.
3. The user's activity on a resource or with another user has a direct or indirect impact on the quality of the related content.

GIAR applies points, collecting and feedback as its basic game mechanics,. Based on points rewarded for each interaction, a level system has been derived that maps a user's progress globally and within the interaction classes or interaction types derived by the interaction taxonomy. Beside points, GIAR rewards users with various awards that they may win for single interactions (medals) or for aggregated interactions (badges). Feedback has been integrated by way of statistics about various aspects of a user's progression and behavior.

6 The qKAI Mashup Framework

According to C. Schroth and T. Janner [125], we see the relation of our needs to service-oriented software design (SOA) as:

"The first major analogy between product design in the fields of Web 2.0 and SOA is the notion of reusing and composing existing resources. Both concepts let users reuse, remix, and enrich existing resources and components to new and potentially higher-level applications. The second commonness is the affinity to collaboration and coupling of remote resources or services. Both Web 2.0 and SOA applications enable the loose coupling of distant and possibly heterogeneous resources. A third apparent resemblance between Web 2.0 and SOA is the shared principle of agility and the support of permanent structural change." [125]

The long-term objective is to embed different types of distributed web resources and services (atomic, simple and composite services) into a knowledge-oriented mashup framework for systematically utilizing distributed web resources and enhancing Open Knowledge and its representation for the user.

The term "Mashup" is defined in Wikipedia [141] as follows:

"In web development, a mashup is a web page or application that uses and combines data, presentation or functionality from two or more sources to create new services. The term implies easy, fast integration, frequently using open APIs (an interface implemented by a software program that enables it to interact with other software) and data sources to produce enriched results that were not necessarily the original reason for producing the raw source data. The main characteristics of the mashup are combination, visualization

and aggregation. Mashup is important to make more useful already existing data, moreover for personal and professional use."

This functionality is exactly what the **qKAI mashup framework** offers for distributed Open Content in interactive knowledge systems and social web applications respectively. To enhance the representation of distributed resources, game based interactivity is a good way to increase user participation, motivation and simplify access to information. Distributed web resources are embedded into web-based games and act as interactive knowledge systems in this way.

Design concepts from service-oriented and mediator/wrapper-based information systems [126] are applied in the system specification of the qKAI mashup framework. We identified three main service categories and packaged them into three service bundles, as interaction, representation and discovery manager, in a mediation layer (see **Figure 35**). To keep the system structure comprehensive and easily extensible, a four-tier layer concept is paired with Rich Client MVC2 paradigms to structure and model the desired service managers and types.

To keep the qKAI application structure flexible, extensible and autonomic, functional subtasks are encapsulated in small web services. Web service interaction follows RESTful Web 2.0 paradigms. Self-descriptive messaging is the most important constraint of REST. It means that every message needs to include all the information necessary in order to understand the message itself. The fundamental advantage of REST over SOAP or CORBA, for example, is that all the service interfaces are the same. There are no differences that require explicit description. Available services and resources are registered in the qKAI data storage according to a broker. In future work, Non-RDF resources can be embedded by converting them to RDF from structured databases.

We divide qKAI functionality into the following two main developer levels:

- **RESTful backend web services** for acquiring, selecting and representing textual and multimedia data. Read and write access to resources is performed over an HTTP protocol according to the GET and POST method. Working at this level means extensive use of a Java Jersey API (JAX-RS specification) to build atomic web services for several subtasks in an effective manner.

- **Rich user interface components** (ui) let the user interact with different kinds of activities. Frontend components are built with AJAX and/or Flash/Flex depending on their type of interactivity.

6.1 qKAI Systems Design

The system design of the qKAI mashup framework is conceptually organized in **four main layers** as a combination of mediator/wrapper concepts [127] [126], service oriented approaches (Internet of Services) and a conventional web application N-tier design. In this section, we explain the components and tasks of the applied layers as shown in **Figure 35**.

The presentation layer implements a General User Interface (GUI) and the logic that goes with it. To fulfill extended MVC2 separation, the mediation layer presents the business logic and controller functionality. We would place the Enterprise Service Bus (ESB) here in a service-oriented way, and the service broker belonging to the discovery manager. The mediation layer acts as middleware connecting available services (service mediation) and other technical components. The definition of "mediation" in qKAI is also interpreted according to Wiederhold [126] as follows:

"A mediator is a software module that exploits encoded knowledge about certain sets or subsets of data to create information for a higher layer of applications."

The data layer meets the model level in the Model View Controller (MVC) pattern and extends it with wrapper services at the wrapper layer to embed various distributed sources. The data layer has to manage hybrid data processing enabling RDF and XML related da-

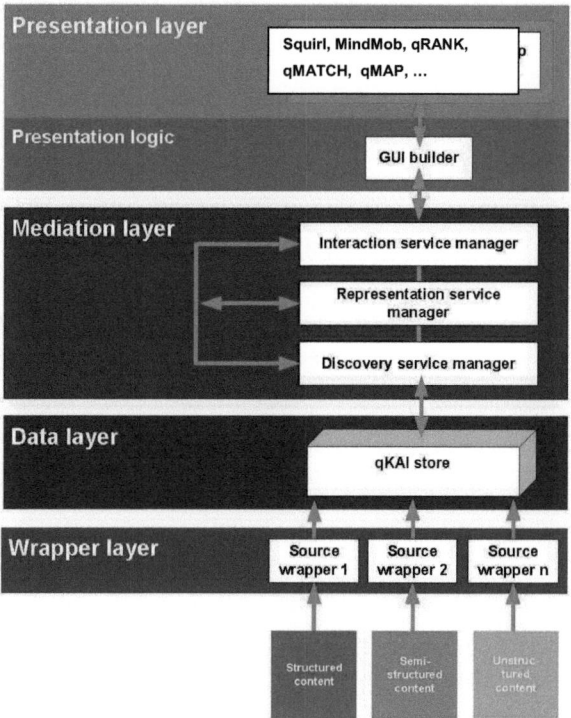

Figure 35: qKAI mashup framework with system layers as conceptual design and development basis

ta, as well as relational database content. Existing data sources are temporarily retained for mediation purposes. qKAI services provide new generated knowledge as open RDF or serialized JSON representation after mediation. The hybrid data layer is explained in more detailed in **Chapter 6.4**.

6.2 Applied Patterns and Techniques

The qKAI mashup framework and dependent web applications are based on the Java Enterprise Edition platform (Java EE) [44], DWR (Direct Web Remoting) [128], Spring-Framework [129] and JavaScript. Java EE is a platform that enables the development of Java based software running on application servers like Apache Tomcat [130]. The qKAI mashup framework makes extensive use of the Java REST JAX-RS reference implementation (Jersey) [45].

The Spring-Framework is an open-source Java platform which facilitates the development of Java EE based web applications first and foremost by decoupling application components into models, views (JSPs) and controllers (servlets) therefore it enables the development according to the model-view-controller architectural style. DWR is a Java library that enables communication between JavaScript and Java classes via asynchronous HTTP requests. JavaScript is used to make the application and its interface more usable and dynamic without the need for a user to reload pages with asynchronous communication.

For mapping between XML documents and Java objects, the Java architecture for XML binding JAXB [131] is used. This programming interface allows the appropriate Java classes to be generated using the XML schema definition, and the serialization of Java object tree structures in XML schema instances/XML documents (marshalling), as well as the deserialization of XML Schema instances / XML documents to Java objects (unmarshalling).

6.3 Architecture Overview for Users and Agents

Figure 36 gives a summary of qKAI's main components, stakeholders and data store. qKAI uses an open source relational database management system MySQL [132] to store acquired resources, resource annotations, rewarded user interactions, stats, rewards and general data in a database. In order to enhance performance of ex-

6 The qKAI Mashup Framework

ecuting commands to the database, connections are cached in a connection pool since opening database connections is costly and may decrease performance, especially in database-driven web applications with multi- user or multi-agent requests.

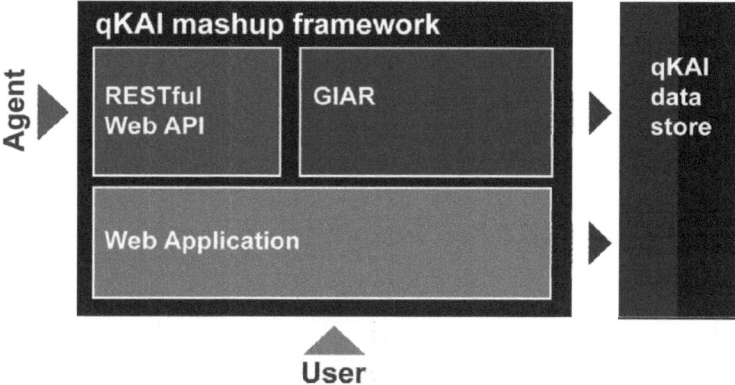

Figure 36: qKAI architecture outline

The GIAR Config file is an XML file that stores configurations for the global rewarding system presented in the next section. It contains the (social) interaction taxonomy illustrated in **Chapter 5.2.2**, enriched with the information needed for the rewarding system. We have identified two stakeholders that access qKAI in different ways. Users access qKAI via its web application interface by creating accounts and logging in web applications like Squirl or MindMob. Agents (in terms of computer programs) access qKAI via its RESTful web API by making an HTTP request.

Finally, GIAR is responsible for rewarding user interactions that may be logged via the RESTful web API or via a web application like Squirl in **Chapter 7.1**. In the following chapters, the main components of qKAI are explained in more detail, as well as the hybrid data layer, the GIAR configuration and tag ranking mechanisms.

6.4 Hybrid Data Layer

The qKAI knowledge representation consists of RDF graphs and superior metadata about them. Existing graphs outside of qKAI are first stored as links to the origin source in the qKAI service and source repository by using the Uniform Resource Identifier (URI) or Uniform Resource Locator (URL) of a SPARQL endpoint like *http://dbpedia.org/sparql*.

Newly generated information is stored separately and is sustainable at the qKAI data layer. The data processing concept contains a persistent, relational database component, flexible representation (RDF, JSON) and temporary fetching of working data during discovery and enrichment. Linked Data concepts [9] enable persistent, resource-related storage, change management and non-redundant, context aware data processing by interlinking identifiable distributed resources. qKAI services generated knowledge about available sources is additionally stored in MySQL and can be represented as Linked Data on demand.

Figure 13 in **Chapter 5.1.2** illustrated how the qKAI data layer embeds Linked Open Data resources and represents its data store as another node in the Linked Open Data cloud. Following the Linked Data keynote and the overall desire of next generation web applications, different, distributed RDF stores should be combined on demand. The qKAI data layer buffers relevant resources in a traditional, relational database structure, to allow adequate performance of a user's requests, optimal reuse and the ability to process and annotate the acquired content further.

This chapter introduces **qKAI data management** based on the concept that every RDF resource can be transferred into a relational database structure and vice versa. **DBpedia** [16] is used as an exemplary knowledge base accessed via its SPARQL endpoint to demonstrate first results while building the hybrid qKAI data store out of distributed web resources.

The main criteria for the qKAI data store are ease of use, affordability, scalability reusability, mediation capability and representation of acquired resources of different kinds and varying provenance. Points of Interest are deployed to give a starting point into a user's knowledge base or further applications and to partially update the qKAI data store on demand in an effective way.

6.4.1   qKAI Resource Annotator

Due to its many positive features (many resources, great topic, extensive ontology, many links to other knowledge bases), DBpedia is (see **Chapter 2.3**) an excellent basis as a central resource collection. For every resource requested an equivalent qKAI resource has to be created in the qKAI data store referencing the information from DBpedia. This is a partial abandonment of the qKAI resource annotator. The data from DBpedia is acquired and included by the DBpedia lookup service, which runs a keyword search, and by direct resource URI requests. For each distributed resource a qKAI Uniform Resource Identifier (URI) is provided – which we refer to as a web link or address in everyday language. Web applications can access qKAI resources to explore or add further resources and annotations using simple HTTP requests. Based on Google's profile, ID user resources can also be created.

The purpose of the qKAI resource annotator and qKAI knowledge base is the reuse of its data and annotation in other web applications. The advantage of the qKAI resource annotator is its ability to write access to distributed resources.

The approach to designing residual web services is aptly described by the following four questions:

1. What resources are available in the qKAI mashup framework?
2. What representations provide a resource?

3. What methods are useful to a resource?
4. What HTTP status codes are needed in response to a request to a resource?

More details and examples of the derived web services of the qKAI resource annotator can be found in **Chapter 6.8.1**.

6.4.2 qKAI Data Access Objects (DAOs)

qKAI uses Data Access Objects [133] (DAOs) to manage database access. DAOs are abstract interfaces that encapsulate access to a data source and therefore enable its replacement without the need to change the code that accesses the data source. Since qKAI uses a MySQL database for data management, abstract DAOs have been implemented to MySQL's database management system [132]. **Table 11** illustrates the DAOs used within qKAI.

DAO	Description
UserDAO	Contains queries to execute user-specific database operations, like inserting user interactions or updating user level states
StatsDAO	Contains queries to retrieve various statistics about users, like user rankings or activity distributions
AppDAO	Interactions are executed in applications and this DAO provides access to application-specific data
ResourceDAO	Contains resource-specific queries
InteractionDAO	Contains queries to store interaction-specific data

Table 11: qKAI Data Acess Objects (DAOs)

DAOs are not accessed directly; they are accessed by using an abstract DAOFactory class. Via the DAOFactory, one chooses which database-specific implementation of the DAOFactory to use for database access operations and its implementation is also responsible for establishment the connection to a data source. The abstract

DAOFactory depicted in excerpts in **Listings 5 and 6** shows a fraction of its MySQL implementation.

```
public abstract class DAOFactory {

    /** MySQL DAOFactory */
    public static final int MYSQL = 1;

    // DAOs supported by the factory.
    public abstract InteractionDAO getInteractionDAO();
                    [... other DAOs ...]

    /**
     * Returns a specific DAOFactory.
     * The provided parameter determines which DAOFactory to return.
     */
    public static DAOFactory getDAOFactory(int whichFactory){
        switch (whichFactory) {
        case MYSQL:
            return new MysqlDAOFactory();
        default:
            return null;
        }
    }
}
```

Listing 5: qKAI DAO factory

```
public class MysqlDAOFactory extends DAOFactory {

    // Create a data source and set it up
    private static DataSource ds = null;
    static {
        [... database driver loading ...]
        ds = setupDataSource();
    }

    // Sets up a connection pooling data source.
    private static DataSource setupDataSource() {
        [... code to create a pooling data source ...]
        return dataSource;
    }

    // Creates a connection to the data source.
    public static Connection createConnection() throws SQLException{
        return ds.getConnection();
    }

    @Override
    public InteractionDAO getInteractionDAO() {
        return new MysqlInteractionDAO();
    }

            [... other DAOs ...]
}
```

Listing 6: qKAI MysqlDAOFactory

6.5 GIAR Configuration

A lot of games use configuration files to configure certain aspects of a game and sometimes users may edit these configuration files to adapt the game to personal preferences. GIAR also uses a configuration file, the GIAR Config file, to configure certain aspects of its rewarding system. During system startup, this configuration is loaded by the GIAR Config Loader (see **Figure 20** in **Chapter 5.2.4**) and stored in the GIAR Config. The GIAR Config contains information about currently rewarded interactions, how many points they earn, if they award medals, to which interaction class and type they belong and it also contains configurations of all the level types presented in **Chapter 5.2.5**.

The GIAR Config File is based on XML and basically contains the (social) interaction taxonomy depicted in **Chapter 5.2.2**, **Figure 19** which has been enhanced with the aforementioned information and configurations. **Listing 7** outlines the basic structure of the GIAR Config file which will be presented more precisely in the following chapters.

6 The qKAI Mashup Framework

```xml
<?xml version="1.0" encoding="UTF-8"?>
<giarconfig xmlns="http://www.squirrl.org/giar">
    <levelconfig <!-- ...level configuration... --> />
    <user-resource>
        <levelconfig <!-- ...level configuration... --> />
        <create>
            <levelconfig <!-- ...level configuration... --> />
            <!-- interactions within this interaction-type -->
        </create>
        <edit>
            <levelconfig <!-- ...level configuration... --> />
            <!-- interactions within this interaction-type -->
        </edit>
        <rate>
            <levelconfig <!-- ...level configuration... --> />
            <!-- interactions within this interaction-type -->
        </rate>
        <explore>
            <levelconfig <!-- ...level configuration... --> />
            <!-- interactions within this interaction-type -->
        </explore>
    </user-resource>
    <user-user>
        <levelconfig <!-- ...level configuration... --> />
        <one_way_interaction>
            <levelconfig <!-- ...level configuration... --> />
            <!-- interactions within this interaction-type -->
        </one_way_interaction>
        <two_way_interaction>
            <levelconfig <!-- ...level configuration... --> />
            <!-- interactions within this interaction-type -->
        </two_way_interaction>
    </user-user>
</giarconfig>
```

Listing 7: Basic structure of the GIAR Config file

On each level of the interaction taxonomy represented in the GIAR configuration file, a <levelconfig>-element defines the properties needed for the level calculation as illustrated in **Chapter 5.2.5**. In **Listing 7, line 3**, properties for the global level are being set. **Listing 7, lines 5** and **24** contain settings for both class levels and settings for all skill levels are being set in **Listing 7, lines 7**, **11**, **15**, **19**, **26** and **30**.

A level configuration for the user-user class level is depicted in **Listing 8**. The name attribute is used to define a fancy name for the level and the other attributes (const1, level1, level2, level3) define values for the corresponding parameters of the level calculation.

6 The qKAI Mashup Framework

```
1 <levelconfig name="Socializer" const1="10" level1="440" level2="880" level3="2200" />
```

Listing 8: Configuration of the user-user interaction class level

Both interaction classes are being created in **Listing 7, lines 4** and **23**. **Listing 7, lines 6, 10, 14, 18, 25** and **29** contain the definition of their interaction types. Each interaction type element in turn contains a list of <interaction> elements defining the interactions belonging to it, as well as how many points they earn. **Listing 9** illustrates the definition of a tag interaction with an optional list of medals that Squirl awards for this interaction. A <medal> element contains attributes defining its type (bronze, silver or gold) and the number of interactions to be executed in order to win the corresponding medal.

```
1 <interaction name="tag" points="20">
2     <medal type="bronze" numberOfInteractions="10" />
3     <medal type="silver" numberOfInteractions="30" />
4     <medal type="gold" numberOfInteractions="70" />
5 </interaction>
```

Listing 9: Configuration of the user-user interaction class level

As mentioned before, the taxonomy and all configurations are stored in the **GIAR Config** and it preserves the taxonomy by a corresponding coupling of interaction related model types, which is illustrated in **Figure 37**.

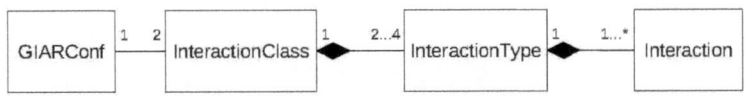

Figure 37: Coupling of interaction related model types

The **GIARConf object** contains references to both interaction classes. Each InteractionClass object contains a list of its interaction types, which in turn have an identifying reference to their interaction class. The InteractionType class also contains an enumeration (Type enum) of all possible interaction types: create, edit, rate, explore, one-way and two-way. In addition to a reference to one of these types, each InteractionType object contains a list of Interaction objects and they in turn have an identifying reference to its InteractionType. Therefore, each interaction is distinctly identified by its interaction type and interaction class. **Listings 10** to **13** depict this coupling via excerpts of their corresponding Java classes.

```java
public class InteractionClass {

    /** interaction-types contained in this interaction-class */
    private List<InteractionType> interactionTypes =
                        new ArrayList<InteractionType>();
    [... other methods and fields ...]
}
```

Listing 10: InteractionClass (excerpt)

```java
public class InteractionType {

    public enum Type{
        CREATE,
        EDIT,
        RATE,
        EXPLORE,
        ONE_WAY_INTERACTION,
        TWO_WAY_INTERACTION;
    }

    /** type of this interaction */
    private Type type;

    /** the interaction-class that this interaction-type belongs to */
    private InteractionClass interactionClass;

    /** concrete interactions ({@link Interaction}) that have this interaction-
        type */
    private List<Interaction> interactions = new ArrayList<Interaction>();
    [... other methods and fields ...]
}
```

Listing 11: InteractionType (excerpt)

```
public class GIARConfig {

    /** user-resource interaction-class */
    private InteractionClass userResourceIaClass;

    /** user-user interaction-class */
    private InteractionClass userUserIaClass;
    [...other methods and fields...]
}
```

Listing 12: GIARConfig (excerpt)

```
public class Interaction {

    /** The interaction-type that this interaction belongs to */
    private InteractionType iaType;
    [...other methods and fields...]
}
```

Listing 13: Interaction (excerpt)

6.6 Tag Ranking Application Flow

In qKAI, currently Flickr [6] is used as an exemplary knowledge base for images. For details regarding the enabled tag ranking algorithms see **Chapter 5.3.5**.

This chapter presents the search and ranking application flow in qKAI while acquiring images from Flickr for given tags by the user.

First, the search term given by the user is compared with the most popular tags in a Flickr group. All groups that contain the search term as tag are weighted on the frequency of their tags. If looking for groups that follow a clear theme, then the weighting is based on the number of elements with this tagged term divided by all the elements. If one is interested in most of the pictures in a search term, then the occurrence of this term is used as a weighting factor. If we got the group with the most appropriate images, we can do a keyword search within this group and sort the images according to their relevance with qRANK (compare **Chapter 7.3**).

Then we successively take into account the following criteria:

1. The compliance of the user's search term with the group's tags is examined.

Since users usually use commonly known way annotations and not all forms of a term together, the above condition is extended. A user who searches for "church" is also interested in pictures annotated with "churches" and the German translation "Kirchen."

    a. An English translation of the search term is taken into account in the search.

    b. To recognize the similarity between the plural and singular, the Levenshtein metric is applied with a distance of two.

The Levenshtein metric can be applied because we can usually take into account that terms like "Church" and "cherry" are different in more than two places. They are not in a singular-plural relationship and are not together amongst the most used tags found in a group because they represent two very different things.

2. If a query matches one of the top five tags, the groups affected are ranked according to the weighting factor.

If several terms match, the sum of all weights is formed. If the tag list of a group does not contain the search term or the groups are empty, they are weighted with Zero. All groups that are equally weighted are ranked according to a second criterion, in this case, the number of images. If the number of images is also equal, the third criterion that would be taken into account would the number of members. As a result of this procedure, we get a ranked list of the groups.

This method is especially effective if we are searching for general subjects that are found in a wide range of groups. **Table 12** contains a partial list of results for the term "Kirche," which provides a total of 1,551 groups. The column **Flickr rank** in the table gives the position in the list that Flickr (sorted by the relevance) usually returns.

6 The qKAI Mashup Framework

Flickr rank	Rank of the searched term inside a group	Group members	Images	Top 5 tags	Occurence tag Kirche / church	qKAI rank
1	4	24	123	münchen munich architecture kirche church	77	1
2	0	1	0	No tags	0	11
4	1	2	1	kirche parchim	1	10
4	0	1	51	judith thomas moe hochzeit	0	9
8	49	420	2358	jesus christianity hymn chant christ	143	8
9	135	6671	79863	italia italy anticando church roma	14598	7
47	5	1643	23796	church europe cathedral architecture kirche	11447	4
138	2	560	30354	church kirche carving austria österreich	8433	6
245	4	91	2173	church europe cathedral kirche architecture	1280	2
367	3	180	1441	gothic architecture church cathedral england	419	5
448	4	1235	10809	church architecture europe	5217	3

6 The qKAI Mashup Framework

				kirche cathedral		

Table 12: Flickr group analysis for the term "Kirche"

The idea of this group ranking procedure is to find the group with the most relevant images. The **red numbers** in the table represent the rank derived from our method. In the first rank position, both lists are still identical, but the remaining positions differ greatly. Flickr weights many groups with "Kirche" in their top five tags stronger, than groups that do not use the tag "Kirche" at all, or very rarely. The explicit consideration of whether the tags are plural or singular and the inclusion of the English translation of the term returns significantly better results than the standard Flickr search. Since Flickr does not provide the needed data for the approach intentionally, it must first be created. Flickr only allows a maximum of 500 pictures or information per request to download at one time. In order to realize a dynamic and non-redundant storage concept, the idea of the Actor-Concept-Instance model has been implemented. For further implementation details see [124].

The approach discussed in this section allows groups to be ranked according to their relevance. Only term frequencies will be considered, which are calculated from the image tags. The images in the groups are not ranked yet.

In **Chapter 7.3**, the idea for an image ranking game called **qRANK** [124] [134] is presented and explained in detail. It provides important information to **rank the tag list of an image automatically**. This information is then used to sort images according to their relevance.

Narrow folksonomies, like Flickr, have a major disadvantage, which is that they do not allow the frequency distribution of the indexed terms. Therefore, it is not possible to observe the abundance and distribution of tags within a resource. Each tag appears only once, so we do not have simple methods to distinguish between relevant and irrelevant tags. A user can tag his pictures in Flickr with up to 75 keywords. In general, the tags are chosen arbitrarily.

For further details about embedding qKAI's group ranking algorithm into its own applications, see the qKAI API.

6.7 qKAI Online Community Models

qKAI incorporates 28 models representing concepts that are crucial for GIAR and the web application used to build an online community like Squirl [46] or MindMob introduced in **Chapter 7**. The models are separated into **interaction**, **level**, **stats** and **general models** all having different conceptual priority with respect to the qKAI mashup framework and the web applications they are based on.

Most models do not contain any logic and can therefore be referred to as JavaBeans [139] that basically store domain specific data via member variables and their respective access operations. Some models have been annotated with JAXB annotations [131] JAXB is an acronym derived from Java Architecture for XML Binding. JAXB is a Java framework that allows developers to map Java objects to an XML representation and vice versa [131]. Mapping XML files to Java objects is called unmarshalling and is mostly done by compiling an XML schema. Mapping Java objects to an XML representation is called marshalling and the aforementioned JAXB annotations are used to specify the desired XML output. **Table 13** outlines the different model types and their characteristics with respect to Squirl.

6 The qKAI Mashup Framework

Model-type	Description
interaction	Represent concepts from the (social) interaction taxonomy presented in section 3.5 and further capture properties and methods related to rewarding features implemented in GIAR
level	GIAR incorporates a game-like level system based on points and theses models represent concepts needed for its implementation
stats	These models capture various statistics about user interactions and are used to provide feedback via Squirrl's REST API or the web application interface
general	Represent general concepts within Squirrl like users, resources or rewards.

Table 13: Model types used in qKAI (especially Squirl)

6.8 qKAI REST API Examples

The following examples of the qKAI's REST API are logically separated into three types of services:

- Resource annotation
- Interaction logging
- Interaction stats services

The resource annotation services allows requesting of Linked Open Data and write access to enrich resources by semantic annotation as outlined in **Chapter 5.1.2**.

Agents, referred to as apps, may reward (and therefore log) user interactions through interaction logging services. With respect to the feedback types introduced in **Chapter 5.2.6**, these services return information about each logged activity. The purpose of the second service type, the interaction stats services, is to offer feedback on a user's statistics and rankings.

6.8.1 Resource Annotation Services

Derived from the requirements and specification of the REST architectural style, **Table 14** contains the resource and interface description for the qKAI resource annotator:

Resources	Representation	Methods	Status codes
./subjects	HTML/XML	GET – request list with qKAI subjects	200 – Ok 202 – No content 500 – Internal Server Error
		No POST necessary	
./subjects/{subject}	HTML/XML	GET – request a subject	200 – Ok 404 – Not found 500 – Internal Server Error
		POST – annotate a subject with annotation object	200 – Ok 400 – bad request 500 – Internal Server Error
./keywordlookup	HTML/XML	GET – keyword search for subjects	200 – Ok 202 – No content 400 – Bad request 500 – Internal Server Error
./	HTML/XML	GET – web service start page and description	

Table 14: Resource and interface description for the qKAI resource annotator

Each resource (referred to internally as subject) can be addressed via a URI. The resource "subjects" provides the list of subjects located in the qKAI database for an HTTP GET request. The resource "subject" represents a single subject and is a sub-resource of the subject's resource. In this way, the hierarchical structure of the list and list items is transmitted to the resources or URI structure. While the GET method returns a subject, the POST method can be used to add an annotation to on a subject. The resource "keywordlookup" provides a service to look up keywords. A GET on this resource with appropriate parameters returns a list of matching subjects. The ad-

6 The qKAI Mashup Framework

dressable resources via HTTP requests with the supported methods form the interfaces of the annotation web services.

The DBpedia Linked Open Data cloud presented in **Chapter 2** is an excellent example resource because of its positive characteristics, which have already been mentioned (many resources, great topic, extensive ontology, many links to other knowledge bases): Every occurring resource in DBpedia can be annotated by the qKAI resource annotator, therefore an equivalent referencing resource is created in the qKAI database. REST-based HTTP requests (see **Table 13**) are used to access these resources and resource annotations can be added. The purpose of the qKAI resource annotator and its knowledge base is the use of its data and annotation in other applications (see preceding chapters). These applications can make use of the XML representation format of resources. The following section describes packages and classes of the qKAI resource annotator (for details, see the qKAI API).

- **Resources**: The classes of this package allow performing operations on available resources. They implement the web services interfaces. These classes define both the relative URL paths that accept HTTP requests and the HTTP methods for representations of input and output.
- **Controller:** The classes in this package include the logic and build the internal interface between the resource classes and the data model.
- **Model:** This package contains the classes that define the data model.

The class structure is defined as follows in **Table 15:**

Package	Resources
Classes	ResourceAnnotatorResource SubjectsResource SubjectResource KeywordLookupResource ResourceUtil

Table 15: Class structure of the qKAI resource annotator services (resources)

6 The qKAI Mashup Framework

Each resource class includes methods that are assigned to a specific HTTP request method. There is one method per http request method and format for each representation. The class SubjectResource contains the following methods for example:

- **getSubject**: Accepts HTTP GET requests that expect a resource representation in XML format in the HTTP response.
- **getSubjectHTML**: Accepts HTTP GET requests that expect a resource representation in HTML format in the HTTP response.
- **annotateSubject**: Accepts HTTP POST requests, which deliver an annotation in XML format and returns a subject resource representation in XML format.
- **annotateSubjectHTML**: Accepts HTTP POST requests, which deliver an annotation as parameter and returns a subject resource representation in HTML format.

Referring to **Table 14,** there are similar methods defined for each HTTP request and representation format in other resource classes. Another important feature of the resource classes is the relative path names under which, dissolved by the Jersey framework to a full URI, the resources on the Internet are addressed. In **Table 14**, the relative paths are already given. A special feature will be given for the subject resource. Subject is a sub-resource of the Subject list. A call to a subject resource (path:. / Subjects / {subject name}) is received by the subjects resource and passed through a sub-resource locator method to the subject of resource class, specifying the requested subject Name. ResourceUtil is a helper class only to offer helper methods that are needed by some resource classes.

Package	Controller
Classes	SubjectService DBPediaService GoogleIDService

Table 16: Class structure of the qKAI resource annotator services (controller)

6 The qKAI Mashup Framework

The service classes in the controller package process the logical tasks that are expressed by HTTP requests.

Most of the tasks such as searching and supplying a subject or adding an annotation to a subject is coordinated by the SubjectService class. The class DBPediaService implements functions that access the DBpedia knowledge base. This includes, for example, the resource location and extraction of data from these. Analogous to the class DBpediaService with GoogleIDService there is a class that implements the functions that will access Google Profiles. This class creates user subjects from the subject service.

Package	Model
Classes	SubjectList Subject Annotationen KeywordSearchResult (schema1.xsd)
DBpedia	ArrayOfResult ObjectFactory

Table 17: Class structure of the qKAI resource annotator services (model)

The model package combines all the classes to model the resources the qKAI resource annotator is working with, i.e. that is, especially the subject resource that presents a resource according to the principles of the Semantic Web. Annotation is an element of a subject. SubjectList and KeywordSearchResult contain a list of the requested subjects. The package also contains the XML schema definition from which the classes were generated using JAXB [131]. Sub-package DBpedia are classes that are required by DBpediaService to serialize the DBpedia resources from the DBpedia knowledge base. More background information is available in **Chapter 6.4.1**.

6.8.2 Interaction Logging Services

As we mentioned in **Chapter 5.2.4** and **6.5**, we also want to offer the ability to embed global interaction rewarding (GIAR) into web applications. Therefore, the following API services are implemented:

For each interaction-type within the (social) interaction taxonomy outlined in **Chapter 5.2.1**, a corresponding log service is available. In other words, each log service logs only those interactions that have the respective interaction type. This not only ensures that logged interactions have the right interaction type, it also ensures that they have the right interaction class, since each interaction-type is distinctly identified by its interaction class. According to the REST architectural style for web services, each log service corresponds to a resource that can be accessed via its URI. As the logging services only differ in their interaction type, each one of them has been realized as a sub-resource to the InteractionLogController root-resource listed in **Listing 14**. A root resource is a Java class that has been annotated with a @Path attribute and each method within this class that has been annotated with a @Path attribute corresponds to a sub-resource. This enables common functionality for a number of resources to be grouped together and potentially reused. [46]

```
1 @Path("/squirrl/interaction/")
2 public class InteractionLogController {
3
4         [... logging services ...]
5
6 }
```

Listing 14: InteractionLogController root resource

All sub-resources share the same (relative) base URI defined by their root resource and this base URI will be extended by the @Path attribute defined for each sub-resource. As already mentioned, all logging services correspond to one interaction type, therefore the InteractionLogController in **Listing 14** contains six sub-resources, one for each interaction type within the interaction taxonomy. **Listing 15**

6 The qKAI Mashup Framework

outlines those sub-resources along with their @Path attribute and other annotations needed to define their properties.

```
@Path("/squirrl/interaction/")
public class InteractionLogController {

    @GET
    @Path("create/{interaction}")
    @Produces(MediaType.APPLICATION_JSON)
    public String logCreateActivity ([...parameters...]) {[...body...]}

    @GET
    @Path("edit/{interaction}")
    @Produces(MediaType.APPLICATION_JSON)
    public String logEditActivity ([...parameters...]) {[...body...]}

    @GET
    @Path("rate/{interaction}")
    @Produces(MediaType.APPLICATION_JSON)
    public String logRateActivity ([...parameters...]) {[...body...]}

    @GET
    @Path("explore/{interaction}")
    @Produces(MediaType.APPLICATION_JSON)
    public String logExploreActivity ([...parameters...]) {[...body...]}

    @GET
    @Path("communication/simple/{interaction}")
    @Produces(MediaType.APPLICATION_JSON)
    public String logOneWayCommunicationActivity ([...parameters...]) {[...body...]}

    @GET
    @Path("communication/complex/{interaction}")
    @Produces(MediaType.APPLICATION_JSON)
    public String logTwoWayCommunicationActivity ([...parameters...]) {[...body...]}
}
```

Listing 15: Interaction logging service

All logging services process HTTP GET requests as defined by the @GET annotation. The @Produces annotation determines the generation of JSON representations of their resources. The @Path annotation of the sub-resources contains a path parameter specifying the interaction to be logged for the corresponding interaction type. The logging services share almost the same set of parameters that requesters must provide in order to log user interactions successfully. These parameters can be provided as path parameters, annotated with @PathParam, or they can be sent as query parameters annotated with a @QueryParam that needs to be appended to the request URI. **Listings 16** and **17** outline the required parameters by

6 The qKAI Mashup Framework

the method signature of two logging services, one logs interactions within the create interaction type and the other logs interactions within the two-way interaction type. [46]

```
@GET
@Path("create/{interaction}")
@Produces(MediaType.APPLICATION_JSON)
public String logCreateActivity(
                @PathParam("interaction") String interaction,
                @QueryParam("user") String userId,
                @QueryParam("app") String app,
                @QueryParam("resource") String resource)
                {[...body...]}
```

Listing 16: Interaction logging service for create activities

```
@GET
@Path("create/{interaction}")
@Path("communication/simple/{interaction}")
public String logOneWayCommunicationActivity(
                @PathParam("interaction") String interaction,
                @QueryParam("user") String userId,
                @QueryParam("app") String app,
                @QueryParam("partner") String partner)
                {[...body...]}
```

Listing 17: Interaction logging service for for one-way activities

As already mentioned, the interaction parameter specifies the interaction to be logged having the respective interaction type and the user parameter specifies the user who has executed the interaction. For security reasons, this user must be known to Squirl, therefore it must be the username of a user having a Squirl account. The same holds true for the app parameter, which identifies an application by its API key. Squirl defines an API key for each app that wants to reward user interactions via the logging services and thereby prevents arbitrary interaction logging for unknown users or unknown apps. The resource and partner parameters are optional and specify a resource for user-resource interactions or a communication partner for user-user interactions. The procedure for logging interactions is the same for all logging services:

1. The service forwards the request to the InteractionLoggerAndStats-Provider, which logs the interaction and preprocesses related statistics.

2. The InteractionLoggerAndStatsProvider checks if the passed parameters are valid, i.e. if a user with the given username exists, if an app with the given API key exists and if the passed interaction is currently supported within the corresponding interaction type.

   a. If any of the passed parameters are not valid, a JSON object is created that contains an error message describing the problem.

   b. If all passed parameters are valid, the interaction will be stored in the database and the following statistics will be returned as a JSON object.

   c. Statistics about the interaction, such as its name, interaction type and class, how many points it earns, how often it has been executed and if a medal has been unlocked. Statistics about each level affected, such as a user's current level, if the user has leveled up, the total number of points in the respective set of interactions and how many points a user needs to reach the next level, are generated.

6 The qKAI Mashup Framework

3. All created JSON objects are wrapped into one JSON object, which is returned to the requesting app. **Listing 18** shows an example of such a JSON object. **Figure 38** illustrates the logging procedure as a sequence diagram. [46]

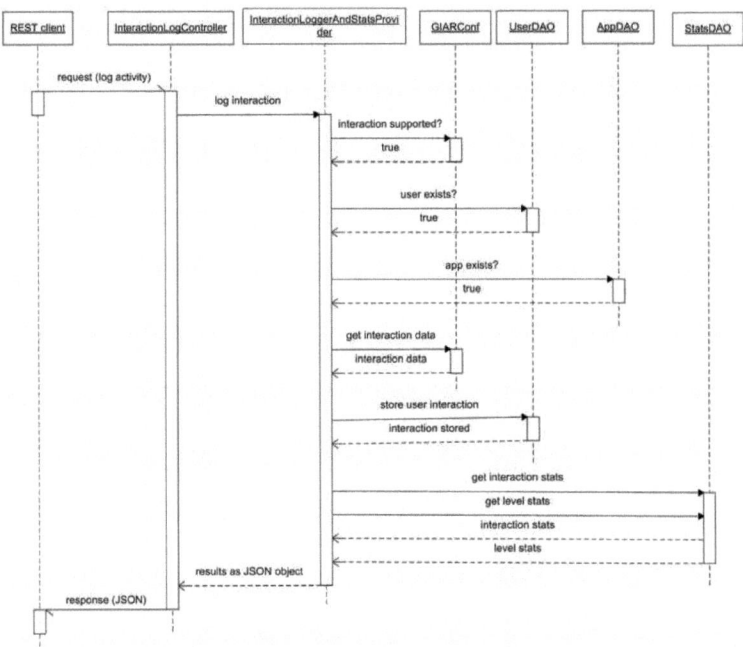

Figure 38: Interaction logging sequence

6 The qKAI Mashup Framework

```
{
"class_level":
        {"level_name":"Surfer Level",
        "level":6,
        "level_up":false,
        "points_to_next_level":13240,
        "points":3640},
"skill_level":
        {"level_name":"Editor Skill Level",
        "level":8,
        "level_up":false,
        "points_to_next_level":8810,
        "points":1970},
"global_level":
        {"level_name":"Squirrl Level",
        "level":5,
        "level_up":false,
        "points_to_next_level":16865,
        "points":4125},
"interaction"
        {"medal":"null",
        "num_interactions":11,
        "ia_type":"EDIT",
        "name":"tag",
        "ia_class":"user-resource",
        "points":50}
}
```

Listing 18: JSON response to an interaction logging request

The corresponding service call to produce the JSON object depicted in **Listing 18** would look like this:

GET
http://squirl.org/rest/squirl/interaction/edit/tag?user=nick&app=xyz&resource=image

6.8.3 Interaction Stats Services

The interaction stats services offers REST clients various statistics about users and user rankings as leaderboards. As with the logging services, each available stats service is realized as a sub-resource to the StatsContoller root resource listed in **Listing 19**. All services can be accessed via the HTTP Get method and produce either a JSON or XML representation of their resources. Like the logging services, the stats services forward their requests to a StatsProvider that aggregates and preprocesses all the data needed for a response. [46]

6 The qKAI Mashup Framework

```
1 @Path("/squirrl/stats/")
2 public class StatsController {
3         [... stats services ...]
4 }
```

Listing 19: StatsContoller root-resource

Currently Available Stats Services:

getUserStats: user/{username}

Required parameters: username

Optional parameters: —

Response format: XML

Returns statistics about a user's current level state in each level type, which interactions a user has executed so far, how often they have been executed and which medals the user has won for which interaction.

getUserActivityProgress:
progress/user/{username}?period={value}

Required parameters: username, period [allowed values: week, month, year]

Optional parameters: —

Response format: JSON

Returns the number of interactions a user has executed within the given period. Interactions within the current year are grouped by month, and interactions within the current month and week are grouped by the day and week in the corresponding month.

getUserActivityDistribution:
activity/distribution/user/{username}?filter={value}

Required parameters: username, filter [allowed values: classDist, typeDist]

Optional parameters: —

Response format: JSON

Returns the distribution of user interactions, either between both interaction classes [filter=classDist] or between all interaction types [filter=typeDist].

getUserLevelEvolution: ranking/user/{username}

Required parameters: username, filter [allowed values: global, class, skill]

Optional parameters: —

Response format: JSON

Returns the level evolution of a user; this is done for the global level, both class levels, or for all skills. Statistics about level evolutions contain feedback on the current level and total number of points, and how many points a user needs for the current and for the next level.

getUserRewards: user/{username}/rewards

Required parameters: username

Optional parameters: —

Response format: JSON

Returns all awards a user has won.

getUserRank: user/{username}

Required parameters: username

Optional parameters: —

Response format: JSON

Returns all user rankings a user may hold within Squirl, i.e. user's global rank, rankings within both interaction-classes and within all interaction-skills.

getGlobalLeaderboard: leaderboard/global

Required parameters: —

Optional parameters: top

Response format: XML

Returns a global user ranking based on a user's total number of points within Squirl. The ranking can be limited by the top parameter

getUserResourceClassLeaderboad:
leaderboard/class/user_resource
getUserUserClassLeaderboad:
leaderboard/class/user_user

Required parameters: —

Optional parameters: top

Response format: XML

Returns a (limited) user ranking for the userresource (user-user); this is also done for the interaction class, which is based on a user's total number of points within the corresponding interaction class.

getUserResourceSkillLeaderboad:
leaderboard/class/user_resource/skill/{skill}
getUserUserSkillLeaderboad:
leaderboard/class/user_user/skill/{skill}

Required parameters: skill

Optional parameters: top

Response format: XML

Returns a (limited) user ranking for a skill within the user-resource (user-user) interaction class; this is based on a user's total points within the corresponding interaction skill.

getActivityRanking: leaderboard/activities/{period}

Required parameters: period [allowed values: week, month, year]

Optional parameters: top

Response format: XML

Returns a (limited) activity ranking for the given (current) time period; the ranking is based on the number of interactions executed within the provided time period.

getPatronLeaderbord: leaderboard/patron

Required parameters: —

Optional parameters: top

Response format: XML

Returns the (limited) patron ranking for the current month; the ranking is based on the number of interactions executed per day, weighted by their total number of points.

Example: **Listing 20** illustrates the result of an activity leaderboard request for the current year.

Request:

GET http://squirl.org /rest/squirl/stats/leaderboard/activities/year

Response:

```
<leaderboard year="2010" type="activity" period="year">
  <ranking>
    <user name="Mika" rank="1" activities="739"/>
    <user name="fabian" rank="2" activities="454"/>
    <user name="fiwii" rank="3" activities="185"/>
    <user name="wladi" rank="4" activities="22"/>
    <user name="martin" rank="5" activities="4"/>
    <user name="r" rank="6" activities="1"/>
    <user name="Captain_Karacho" rank="7" activities="1"/>
    <user name="Bjoern" rank="8" activities="1"/>
    <user name="james" rank="9" activities="1"/>
  </ranking>
</leaderboard>
```

Listing 20: Response to an activity leaderboard request

6.9 Summary

Chapter 6 presented the systems design and exemplary implementation of the qKAI mashup framework. qKAI enables Social Media mashups (web applications) to query, modify, aggregate, analyze or represent Open Content from distributed web resources like Wikipedia, DBpedia or Flickr.

6 The qKAI Mashup Framework

The qKAI mashup framework offers a **web service collection** to interact with different kind of web resources like text or images. Next to a hybrid data storage concept relying on a relational database (MySQL), qKAI offers a **Global Interaction Rewarding** model to reward any kind of interaction in a web application in a generic, application independent and extensible way. The configuration of GIAR is stored in a XML based configuration file which will be loaded during system startup. This configuration contains information about interactions GIAR rewards, how many points they earn, awards they may unlock and to which interactionclass or interaction type they belong. Furthermore, settings needed for the initialization of Squirl's level system are provided by this configuration file. As an important part of the global rewarding system, a REST API has been implemented.

The qKAI REST API enables web applications to annotate resources, reward user interactions, as well as to request statistics about a user's progression or to request leaderboards that enable social comparability in a basic fashion.

The **Open Content's quality** can be enhanced by tag ranking and rating mechanisms for images in folksonomies (**keyword-oriented group search** and **tag ranking game** qRANK). Qualified qKAI content is available for reuse in higher-layered applications as shown in **Chapter 7.3**.

To make the qKAI functionality freely available for other web applications, qKAI offers an Application Programming Interface (API) like other "mashable" [141] web applications that are reachable by RESTful web services.

At this point, there are first-time examples of different knowledge engineering and user interaction tasks available (compare **Chapter 9.1**), but the API can be extended in any direction. It is a work in progress. The focus of the implementation of this thesis is the "Proof of Concept" and to evaluate the basic principles of the qKAI mashup framework as outlined by the evaluation in **Chapter 8**.

In **Chapter 7**, insight is given into specific application scenarios like Social Communities or evaluation games and use cases relying on the qKAI mashup framework introduced in **Chapter 6**.

7 Applications Based on the qKAI Mashup Framework

To highlight what concepts described are suitable for in detail, we implemented two online communities prototypically, based on the qKAI mashup framework with its data layer and its web service collection.

7.1 Squirl: Social Interaction Rewarding Community

In the past five years, the number of online communities has literally exploded and every community depends on their users as they are the creative power that injects life into the community. In order to run a successful online community, designers need to deal with various challenges.

The first, basic challenge is to win new users, which is much easier these days because of social networks like Facebook [22], with which one can reach many people. Once a community has won active users, it definitely wants to keep them active and this is another great challenge communities need to cope with. Keeping users active is where game design principles and mechanics come into play as games have proven to be successful in user engagement and motivation. More and more web sites use game design principles like points or rewards to keep their users motivated. The effort to incorporate game design principles in a proper way cannot be denied, since just adding points may have little or even no positive effect on a user's' motivation in the long run. The purpose of Squirl is to overcome the need to incorporate game design principles into one's web application and still take advantage of those game design aspects that affect user motivation. In order to achieve this goal, Squirl uses the global interaction rewarding system GIAR, which is both specific and general enough to cover all interactions currently available in (social) web applications. GIAR can be used by any web application via Squirl's RESTful web services, thereby enabling them to reward their users for being active. User activities from various online communities or networks can be logged and used to create various statistics about a user's general interaction behavior in those web applications that they are active in. Furthermore, Squirl offers a social online community where users can share their activities with others, have a look at their activity stats, rankings and awards they have won. Enabling users to socially compare their online activity with others fosters their innate competitive drive, which may result in more activities in those web applications that use Squirl's rewarding system. After all, this is what every web application wants to achieve: keeping their users motivated and active. [46]

7.1.1 Squirl Web Application

The purpose of Squirl's web application is to provide users the opportunity to keep track of their progress, as well as to socially compare themselves with other users. Users can monitor each logged interaction or they may have a look at various statistics about their activities. These statistics are visualized by several diagrams and activity clouds providing users the facility to check out the interactions they execute the most at a glance. Squirl currently supports interactions within Facebook [22], Last.fm [23], Flickr [6] and of course within Squirl itself, that is these applications have an API key that is required for each interaction logging request. In order to facilitate the startup within Squirl, users may import interactions from supported apps. If a user has provided the required account information for supported apps, Squirl prompts them for appropriate information, e.g. it requests Flickr for all photos uploaded by a user and for each uploaded photo an upload interaction will be logged and rewarded. Plan are in works to import interactions from other web applications like Twitter or Youtube, but in the long run, interactions should not be imported, but rather logged by those and other web applications using Squirl's REST API. The prototypical implementation of Squirl's web applications will be presented in the following sections.

7.1.2   Squirl's Start Page

Squirl's start page, depicted in **Figure 39**, illustrates three issues:

- The five latest user activities (left column) — latest rewarded activities
- The five most active users this month (middle column) — ranking is based on the total number of activities per user within the current month
- The top five Squirl users (right column) — ranking is based on the total number of Squirl points per user

Currently, the list containing the five latest activities will only be updated after the page has been reloaded, but it is planned to update this list every couple of seconds in order to make the start page more dynamic by making it less static and more interesting to users.

As already mentioned in **Chapter 3.2.1**, leaderboards have the ability to foster a user's competitive drive and this is basically the purpose of both of the rankings presented on the start page as it hopefully results in more activities within supported apps or even causes users to create accounts within them. [46]

7 Applications Based on the qKAI Mashup Framework

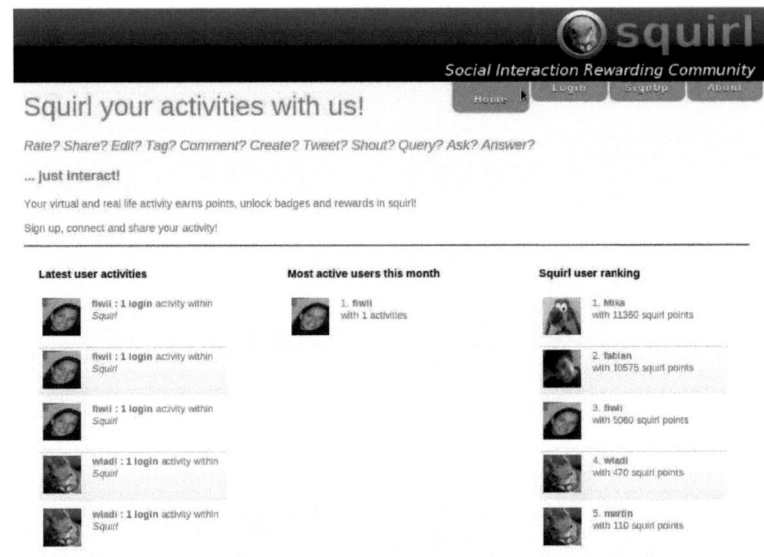

Figure 39: Squirl start page [46]

7 Applications Based on the qKAI Mashup Framework

7.1.3 MySquirl - Squirl User Page

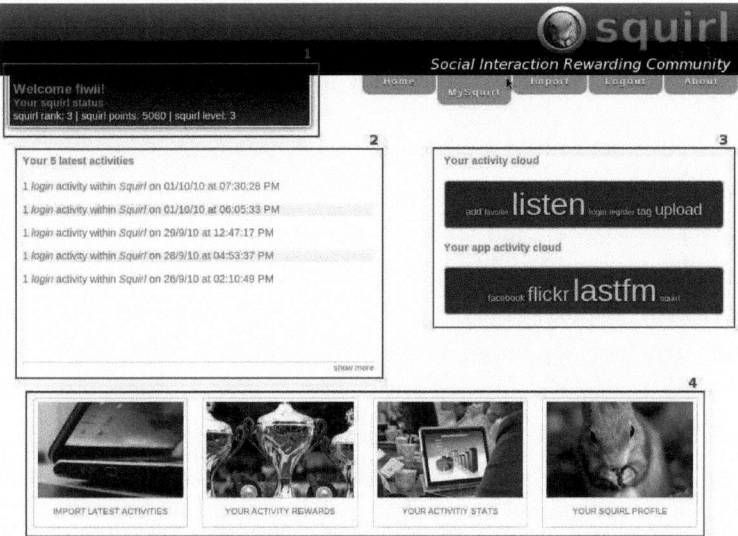

Figure 40: MySquirl — user's personal Squirl page [46]

A user will be forwarded to the MySquirl page after logging in. As depicted in **Figure 40**, this page contains four areas:

1. **Welcome area**: outlines the current Squirl state of a user, i.e. her position within the Squirl ranking (squirl rank), the total number of points she has (squirl points) and which global level she holds (squirl level)

2. **Latest activities area**: outlines the five latest rewarded activities and provides users the opportunity to get a full list of all rewarded activities

3. **Activity clouds area**: displays two activity related clouds: the upper cloud outlines the most rewarded interactions of a user and the lower one outlines those applications a user is most active in or has been most rewarded by

167

4. **MySquirl menu area**: currently offers users four options which will be explained in the following paragraphs (from left to right) — Import Latest Activities, Your Activity Rewards, Your Activity Stats and Your Squirl Profile.

7.1.4 Import Latest Activities

As previously mentioned, Squirl provides the opportunity to import activities from supported web applications and users may regularly import them to keep their Squirl state up to date. This functionality is a temporary solution until other web applications (hopefully) start to reward user activities via Squirl's REST API, so only certain activities within those web applications will be rewarded during an import, e.g. "listening" within Last.fm or "upload" within Flickr.

Figure 41 illustrates the import of latest Flickr photo upload activities of a user by means of a sequence diagram. [46]

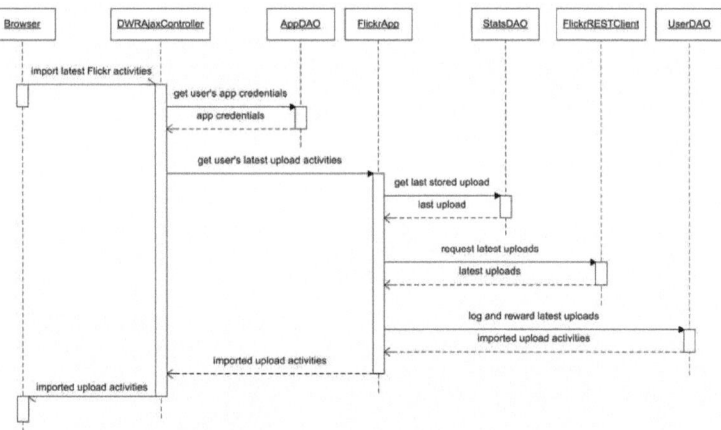

Figure 41: Activity import sequence [46]

7.1.5 Your Activity Rewards

This page displays all awards a user has won so far, grouped by medals for single interactions and badges for aggregated interactions. As illustrated in **Figure 42**, each rewarded medal or badge displays information about its awarding.

 CREATOR of the week 16. August - 22. August 2010
Awarded for having most creator points that week.

Figure 42: Creator of the week badge [46]

7.1.6 Your Activity Stats

This page offers several statistics about a user's Squirl progression and activity distribution. **Figure 43** illustrates statistics currently displayed within this page:

1. **Activity Rankings, Points and Levels**: outlines a user's current ranking, points and level for every level type a user can hold within Squirl

2. **Level and Skill Progress:** plots the completeness (in %) of every level type, indicating how many points a user currently has and needs to reach the next level

3. **Activity Class/Skill Distribution**: summarizes a user's activity distribution between both interaction classes and all interaction skills

4. **Activities this Month/Year**: displays the activity distribution over the current month (grouped by day) and within the current year (grouped by month)

7 Applications Based on the qKAI Mashup Framework

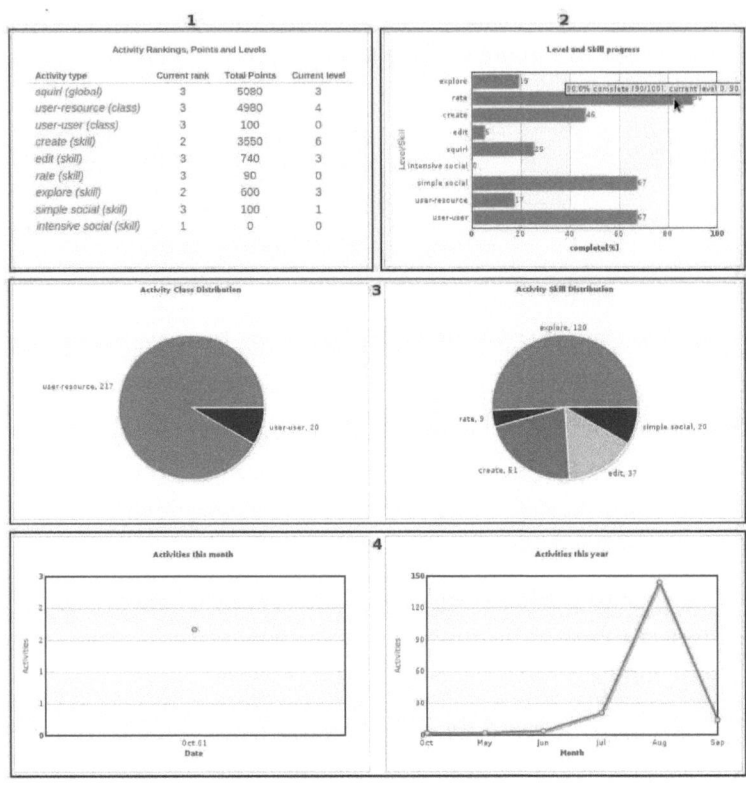

Figure 43: Squirl user stats [46]

7.1.7 Your Squirl Profile

Currently a Squirl user profile only consists of username and an optional photo, but in future, further user properties will need to be stored in order to enable other functionalities like real awards (e.g. a cafe coupon). Furthermore, other user properties will be made public like awards or statistics and this page will offer users the option of defining which properties should be publically available and which should not.

7.1.8 Real Awards

Squirl currently awards virtual rewards like points, medals and badges. A possible advancement related to this part of Squirl would be to award real rewards like coupons for books, travels or for the most popular coffeehouse. Using coupons to assemble real awards seems to be the easiest way as with coupons there is no need for a sales department and there are no limits to the type and purpose of coupons. Furthermore, coupons are not bound by location and can be given out for any venue in any city. Virtual awards offered by Squirl could be mapped to real awards, e.g. if a user unlocks the "Socializer of the week" badge, she may be rewarded with a coupon for a nice restaurant or if someone unlocks the "Explorer of the week" badge it may be rewarded with a travel voucher.

7.1.9 Critical Appraisal

The application of game design principles like points, levels and awards in contexts other than games has proven to be a promising approach in creating user engagement and the test application used for this evaluation has shown that those functionalities need not be incorporated into an application itself, but can be used via qKAI's or Squirl's REST API. Although the evaluation clearly shows that rewarding mechanisms have a positive effect on user behavior and motivation, it is not clear how these behaviors evolve over time. For short-term applications this may not be a problem, but for long running or even "never ending" applications that most web communities or applications wish to be, keeping their users constantly motivated is a life's work. For such applications it is crucial to know how rewarding mechanisms such as the ones Squirl offers affect user behavior in the long run. Squirl offers universal applicable game design principles in order to be used by any other web application and this universality may be a drawback for applications that want to integrate game design principles that are more specifically related to the services they provide.

Currently, interactions are being rewarded just by executing them. No statements are being made about how "good" or "bad" an interaction or its result was. For example, if an application rewards users for making reviews about movies, the rewarding of a review interaction as Squirl supports does not make any statements about how useful a review is with respect to other users reading it, i.e. a "good" review should earn more points than a "bad" review. This problem may indeed result in useless interactions like adding "foreign friends" to Facebook just to earn points for adding interactions and useless interactions again may result in useless (open) content if applications reward creative interactions. In general, arrangements need to be made that prevent users from gaming the system and it must be checked if such arrangements can be made by Squirl or if applications that want to use Squirl's rewarding mechanisms have use them.

7.2 MindMob: A Knowledge Community with Open Content

MindMob is a social educational gaming community based on Open Content. MindMob also relies on the qKAI mashup framework. The Squirl components shown in **Chapter 7.1** like registering, login, profile, leaderboards or the main layout structure are also used in MindMob and the main application structure remains the same.

Next to the common community features and the embedded GIAR component such as the one in Squirl, MindMob offers additional interfaces to interact with Open Content. The users can explore, view, select or even play with distributed resources like DBpedia or Flickr. In the following, a few examples of MindMob use cases and their implementation are given.

qMAP, qMATCH, the SPARQLizer and qRANK are frontend components coupled with qKAI web services that can be deployed inside an online community like MindMob or as smaller stand-alone web applications.

7.2.1 qMAP: A Geo-Coded Visualization of Open Content

Figure 44: qMAP frontend

qMAP [134] [124] is the implementation of a map-based user interface to query, select and edit interlinked web resources. qMAP (see **Figure 44** and **45**) allows the user to filter DBpedia [16] entries and related multimedia content like Flickr images [6], YouTube videos [5] or Last.fm music [23]. Thematically and geographically personalized knowledge views are possible. Knowledge gaming content can be also placed on the qMAP.

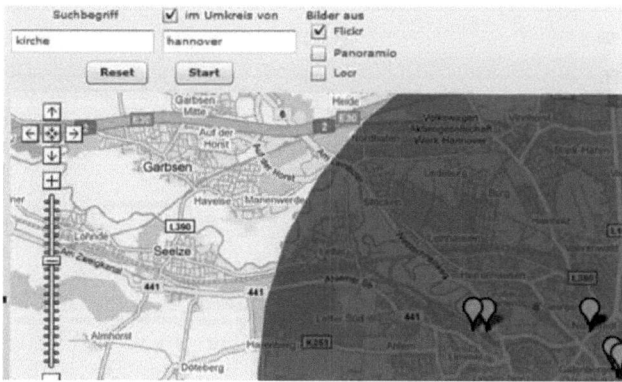

Figure 45: Search, filter and periphery interface of qMAP

7 Applications Based on the qKAI Mashup Framework

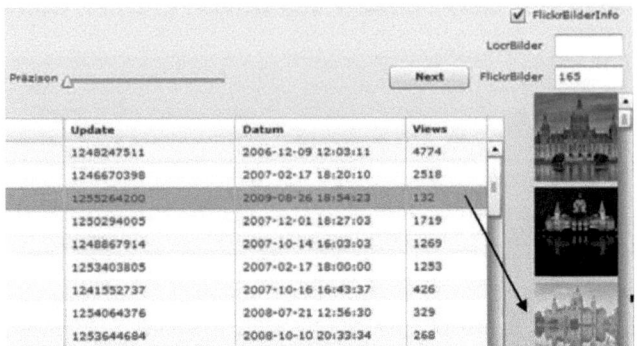

Figure 46: History and interaction protocol of Open Content for statistical analysis behind the qMAP interface.

Qualified Flickr images played first by qRANK are integrated into qMAP too (**Figure 44** and **45**). **Figure 45** shows the periphery search and explore functionality of the qMAP. As shown in **Figure 46**, every user task and interaction is locked in qKAI's history protocol, e.g. update, creation date or views of images are.

The graphical interface of qMAP consists of three different states so users can show or hide individual functions by clicking on the checkboxes. By default, a keyword search in Flickr is set. By checking the "search by country" box, the user can search for images within a certain radius and the checkbox "topic search" allows the user to search by topic. In order to not overload the map with markers, only a maximum of 100 images to each request is used. During the area search for Flickr images, the user has the additional option of setting the radius (in km). The selected area is marked in blue on the map (see **Figure 45**).

7.2.2 qMATCH: An Assignment Quiz with Flickr Content

qMATCH [134] is a prototype of an image term assignment gaming type. First, the user enters a term that he wants to get images about. Then Flickr returns random terms and images and he has to assign

7 Applications Based on the qKAI Mashup Framework

the right term to the right image via a drag and drop assignment (see **Figure 47**).

qMATCH is useful for enhancing language skills, geographical, architectural or historical knowledge. If we use a term-term assignment, a great deal of vocabulary from the various domains can be assessed: assigning English to German translations, assigning buildings to right historical epochs or assigning cities to the right countries.

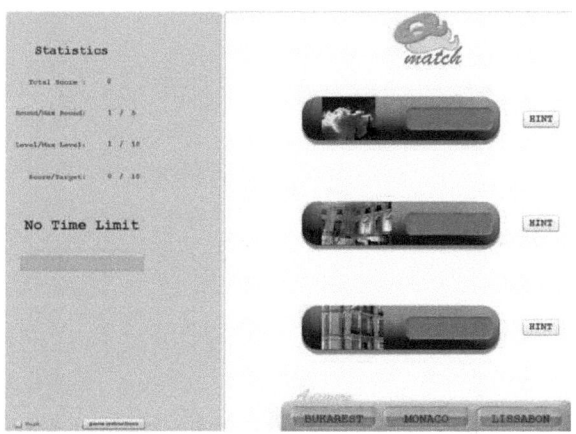

Figure 47: qMATCH text image assignment game

In **Figure 48**, the statistical protocol of a user and his interaction results are shown on Open Content like Flickr images.

7 Applications Based on the qKAI Mashup Framework

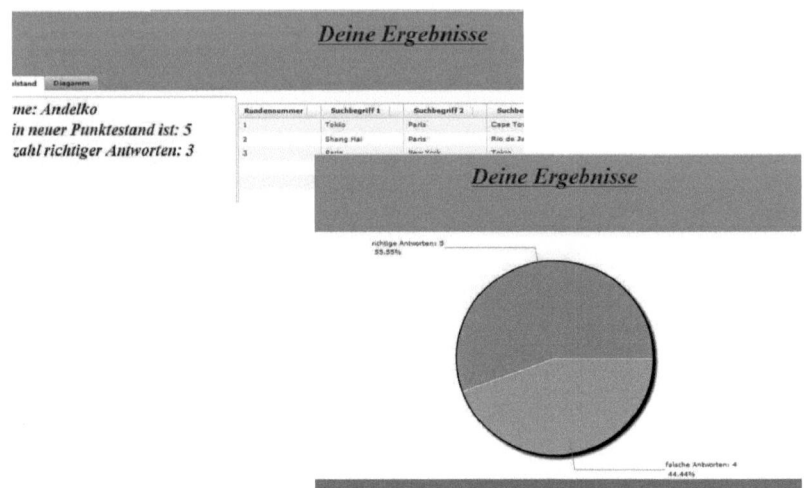

Figure 48: Knowledge game result in qMATCH with own correct answers and aggregated statistics.

7.2.3 DBpedia Guessing Games

DBpedia makes use of Wikipedia categories (SKOS) and YAGO classes [142] to classify its dataset. Concentrating on the predefined categorization, we have a good base on which to build quiz-like **guessing games**. The SPARQL query represents the question that is answered as SPARQL response. qKAI has to represent the SPARQL request as a human capable question, the SPARQL responds with right answers and has to process wrong answers. The implementation is summarized in qKAI under "SPARQLizer," but is still under development and so far, it is only part of the qKAI concept. Questions like "Which of the following cities is not a European capital?" or "Which of the following architects is born in Berlin?" become possible with DBpedia and SPARQL requests. Further examples of questions are: Which German architects are born in Berlin? Which architects are influenced by Mies van der Rohe? Which are the capitals of Europe? Which cities have famous buildings of the gothic era? Which famous people were born in Berlin before 1900?

```
SELECT ?name ?birth ?death ?person WHERE {
    ?person dbpedia2:birthPlace <http://dbpedia.org/resource/Berlin> .
    ?person dbpedia2:birth ?birth .
    ?person foaf:name ?name .
    ?person dbpedia2:death ?death
    FILTER (?birth < "1900-01-01"^^xsd:date) .
}
ORDER BY ?name
```

Which famous people are born in Berlin before 1900?

Listing 21: SPARQL request and qKAI question representation: Which famous people are born in Berlin before 1900?

7 Applications Based on the qKAI Mashup Framework

```
<results distinct="false" ordered="true">
   <result>
      <binding name="name">
         <literal aaa:lang="de" xmlns:aaa="http://www.w3.org/XML/1998/namespace">(August)
Immanuel Bekker</literal>
      </binding>
      <binding name="birth">
         <literal datatype="http://www.w3.org/2001/XMLSchema#date">1785-05-21</literal>
      </binding>
      <binding name="death">
         <literal datatype="http://www.␣␣␣.w3.org/2001/XMLSchema#date">1871-06-07</literal>
      </binding>
```

Immanuel Becker
Abraham Mendelssohn Bartholdy
Achim von Arnim
Adalbert von Preußen
...

Listing 22: SPARQL XML response (excerpt) and qKAI quiz answers representation for the question: Which famous people were born in Berlin

7.3 qRANK: Qualifying and Evaluation Game

With the known methods mentioned in **Chapter 5.3.5** like TF-IDF weighting, we could determine relevance more precisely automati-

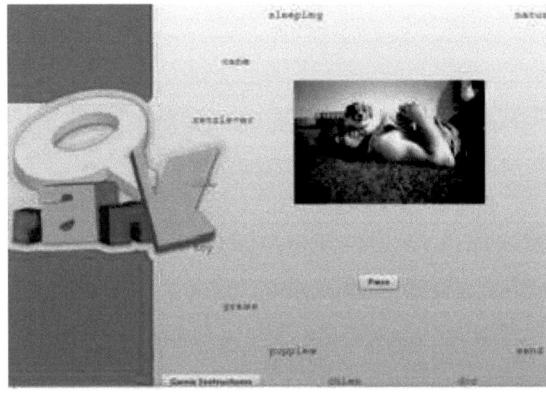

Figure 49: qRANK: A tag rating image text assignment game based on Flickrcontent

cally. Here, we introduce a **different approach**, called qRANK, which allows us to classify the tag list of an image in a **game-based** way. **Figure 49** shows a screenshot of the first qRANK prototype.

This game should investigate how far the process of a player's acquired knowledge in a dynamic ranking can change the tag lists quality. Each pass of the game improves the tag of an image that can be used for further analysis, particularly for improvement of the search list. qRANK is a tag ranking game and can be used as a component in MindMob or as a stand-alone tag rating game.

Most of the analysis so far has dealt with folksonomies that deal mainly with broad folksonomies. The resulting frequency distribution of tags examined is an important indicator to determine the relevance of one tag in reference to the describing ability for a resource. This collective knowledge can provide information about the relevance of a tag. The implementation of the tag rankings (previous section) by a game that implements the idea of the power-law curve would provide additional information for the ranking of images. Most approaches to rank folksonomies are based much more on the FolkRank algorithm [135] or ranking techniques based on particularly elaborate calculations [136]. In this work, the picture's tag list is sorted according to the relevance of its tags. At the same time, the tag list is extended and annotated with new valuable terms. qRANK (see **Figure 49**) queries available web services (almost RESTful) and embeds returned content in a predefined gaming setting. Here we added some algorithms to enhance the precision (relevance) of the search results like an interestingness rating or precision formulas for folksonomies. Additionally, every gaming interaction is logged and ranks played content enabling a user's collective intelligence gradually. Results are stored in qKAI, but are still semantically interlinked with the provenance source in order to not lose the resource's context and also for updating. The techniques used are semantically Linked Data (annotation, interlinking), server-side Java, Adobe Flex/Flash and a MySql database – for representation flexibility. For further implementation details, see [124] and [134].

7.3.1 qRANK: Game Description

The user is presented with a picture and a list of twenty tags. His task is to choose the three most relevant tags that represent the subject of the picture the best in his opinion. Subsequently, the chosen terms are reviewed by the rank in another list, and rewarded with points depending on the rank position of the tags. For each term that is included among the top five tags, the player gets three points. In positions six to ten, the user gets two points and for the positions 11–20 he receives one point. If the term is not included in the list or the rank is below 20, the user does not get any points. The motivation of the player is to achieve the maximum number of points per round to get to the next level. The game consists of ten levels. In each level the player is presented with five consecutive images and can reach a maximum of 45 points. The user needs 20 points to get from level one to two, and increases for each level by 5 points. So to jump from level 6 to level 7 you need full points.

7.3.2 qRANK: Architecture and Backend

Figure 50 describes the components and approximate sequence of qRANK. We downloaded a data set of relevant images to a certain topic from the Flickr web service and stored it in a MySQL database. The information for all the images is recorded in one table. In addition, the related tags that fit best for this subject are saved in another table. In the third table (image tag list) all the tag lists of the images are managed. The image tag list consists of the terms that users have used to describe this picture in Flickr. A fourth table (ranked tag list) is filled dynamically. This is filled at the creation of the game with ten terms of the actual image and a related tag list tag. The ranked tag list contains for each term a counter, which is used to count the frequency of the term.

By chance, the player is presented with a photo and 20 matching tags. The tags will be selected for a specific principle from the tables

7 Applications Based on the qKAI Mashup Framework

"related tag list," "image tag list" and "ranked tag list." This achieves a useful combination of tags. In the very first run of a picture, the length of the "ranked tag list" is set to twenty. While producing the amount of data every tag list will be employed with ten randomly selected tags out of the "related tag list" and "image tag list."

The number of tags in Flickr images is different; many images have less than three tags [138]. If a picture does not have ten tags, as in this case, the missing tags are added from the related tag list. These twenty tags are then stored in the table "ranked tag list" and build the new tag list of images that is sorted dynamically through the game.

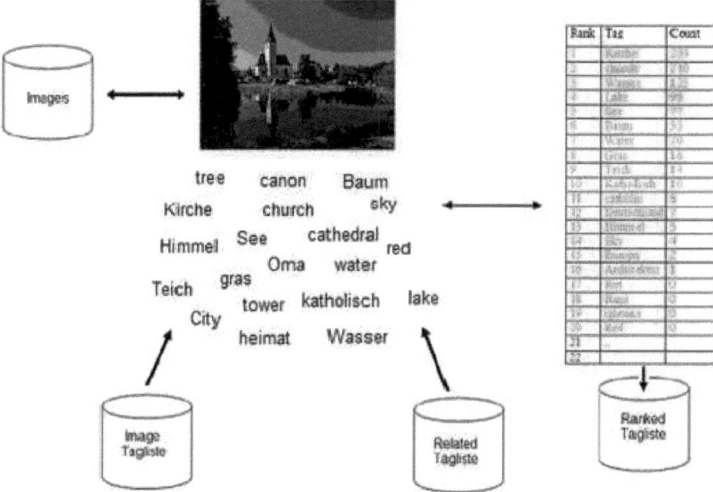

Figure 50: qRANK, a tag rating image text assignment game based on Flickr

7.3.3 qRANK: Game Play

After a player has selected three terms, they are compared with the tag list and awarded with points. Since the first run of the counter of tags starts at zero, an additional condition is defined: If the counter of all terms is the same, the player gets his choice irrespective of the maximum score for that round. From the second pass (for each image) the selection tag list is combined from the first ten tags of the ranked tag list with five randomly selected tags from the "related tag list" and the actual "image tag list." With the selection of the top ten ranked tags from the tag list, we ensure that terms that are more relevant are selected with a higher probability. Even here, it may happen that the actual tag list (image tag list) contains less than five tags. In this case, the remaining tags from the ranked tag list are added. To prevent duplicated tags, the randomly selected tags are compared with the related tag list and the actual tag list of the images with the first ten terms from the ranked tag list. The logic of the game is developed as web services. To get a better overview of the game's flow from the perspective of the player, it is described as follows:

1. The player is presented with a random image and a collection of unsorted tags. He has to choose the most relevant three terms.
2. The chosen three terms will be compared with the ranked tag list.
   a. If they match, he gets (depending on rank of the term) points and the tag counter is incremented.
   b. If the selected tag is not included in the ranked tag list, this is added to it and the counter is set to 1. The player does not receive any points. This ensures that the tag list is ranked and expanded with additional terms. A limit on the maximum number of tags is not set in the game.

However, the maximum number of tags is fixed by the quantity of the tag list and the list of related terms. The primary objective of this game is to evaluate the information gained from the existing tags to an image. Through an extra box, users can also add optional new tags.

7.3.4 qRANK: Ranking the Images

The information, which is calculated from qRANK can easily be converted into a ranking of images. Therefore, qRANK itself is already a precursor of the ranking. The more an image is played, the more meaningful the tag list is. The idea behind this ranking is similar to the group ranking. A picture is evaluated collaboratively and as a result we gain a weighted list of objective tags. The subjective tags that are insignificant for information retrieval drop out automatically. Tags that do not explicitly describe the content of an image and only have a meaning for the person, who assigned them, are not included by the public (the players). The result is a tag list for each image sorted by relevance. The degree of relevance of a term for an image depends on the objective consideration of all the persons who have played this picture.

The result is the basic principle of this tag ranking process. In this procedure, any tag from the ranked tag list, which belongs to the image, is weighted. The weighting consists of the simple calculation of the number of times this tag was chosen, divided by the sum of the possibilities for that selection. The relevance here results from the tag's selection counter in relation to all the other tag selection counters. This finding could be valuable if an image is played with a certain degree of frequency.

7.4 Further Use Cases

There are further use cases in different domains that can be implemented in the future with the help of the qKAI mashup framework. In the following, the main domains are listed where the qKAI mashup framework can be helpful for knowledge engineering and user interaction scenarios.

7.4.1 Information and Guiding Systems Based on Open Content

qKAI's querying, searching, representation or visualization functionalities implemented as web services and web-based frontend components can be reused by further web applications to handle and embed resources like DBpedia and Wikipedia or Flickr, Last.fm and Foursquare. The qKAI data store contains partially enhanced content like more relevant Flickr images than the standard Flickr search interface for example. The resource Annotator can be used in any case as web applications need to be able have write or annotation access to distributed resources.

7.4.2 Enhanced Knowledge Discovery

qMATCH in **Chapter 7.2.2** or the DBpedia guessing game concepts in **Chapter 7.2.3** showed a few first examples of what is possible based on distributed resources in knowledge representation, discovery and game-based knowledge transfer. Ranking games like qRANK in **Chapter 7.3** and further guessing games in all domains easily become possible with classical music content on Last.fm or medical video sequence on YouTube, for example.

7.4.3 Online Monitoring and Social Media Ranking and Analysis

The information gained in Squirl described in **Chapter 7.1** via GIAR is very valuable because it tells us who interacts when and with which kind of resource. Detailed statistical analysis could provide very interesting results concerning product placement, advertising or interaction design and analysis. Personalization, recommendation, and prediction oriented application scenarios become possible this way.

7.5 Summary

In **Chapter 7**, different application scenarios relying on the qKAI mashup framework were shown. qKAI can be used as a tool kit to build RESTful online communities that make extensive use of distributed resources or global activity rewarding. Knowledge engineering tasks like acquisition, inquiry or representation can be handled by qKAI web services. Open Content can be qualified, annotated and enhanced by qKAI web services or user interaction interfaces built upon the qKAI web service collection.

This chapter provided an overview of the main components of **Squirl's** architecture and its centerpiece, the global rewarding system called GIAR.

8 qKAI Evaluation: Proof of Concept

In this chapter we present evaluation results regarding three exemplified application scenarios based on the qKAI mashup framework. For more conceptual background refer to **Chapter 5**.

8.1 Open Content as a Distributed Knowledge Base in Interactive Systems

Up to now, the qKAI knowledge base has contained data from DBpedia and Flickr. Available resources can be annotated by the qKAI resource annotator. User activity in the prototypically implemented online communities Squirl and MindMob enriches the qKAI data store gradually.

The qKAI mashup framework offers the features that would enrich further resources as shown by Flickr, DBpedia or Wikipedia. Applications like Squirl or MindMob embed distributed resources successfully, which allow user interoperation. Applications like qMAP or qRANK can embed a wide range of resources with little effort over a defined and standardized REST API.

8.2 The Impact of User Activity on the Quality of Resources

We have seen that the search for relevant groups and image in folksonomies represents a fundamental problem. Some related approaches have been described in this thesis trying to use the resources metadata (tags to classify). From the analysis of these approaches in this work, new ideas have emerged, which were implemented as a prototype. In this section the effect of the implemented approaches in this work in searching for relevant groups and pictures, are shown. The experiments described below compare the standard keyword search in Flickr with our group ranking method and our game-based approach (qRANK: compare **Chapter 7.3**).

8.2.1 Experiment 1: Group Ranking

The aim of the group ranking procedure is to find the group with the most relevant photos according to a topic or term. These are the groups sorted by topic relevance. To compare the method with the search for relevant groups in Flickr, we stored the term "Kirche" from 100 groups with information about the images, tags and users in a MySql database. The groups search on this term found 1,640 groups at the time of the experiment. To download all the required information over the Flickr API, we have to provide several queries for one group. Unfortunately, the Flickr API did not have the ability to determine the occurrence of a specific identifying tag at the time of this work. Therefore, an additional methodology was created to determine the frequency distribution of tags within a group. We used 100 groups with their 100 most used tags for this. A data set of a million images and over 100 thousand most used tags emerged out of this. To optimize the performance of the database query, the set of tags was reduced to the 100 most used tags per group. The groups were selected as follows: Fifty of the groups were also the first 50 returned by Flickr, and the other half were randomly selected groups from the rest of the crowd.

8.2.2 Result Experiment 1

Figure 51 represents the number of relevant images of the first 20 groups that Flickr provides on the query "Kirche," compared with the process of this work. The red bars describe the results from Flickr and the green bars, the results with the group rankings from this work. The first eight groups in Flickr together provide a total **of 100 images** for the search term. With the group ranking procedure, in the first position, we have a group with **5,262 images.**

8 qKAI Evaluation: Proof of Concept

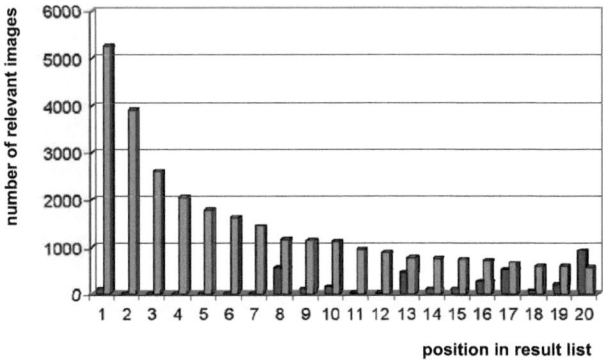

Figure 51: Results of the Flickr group rating approach ranking by the number of relevant images

Considering that Flickr has all of its data available and here we included only 100 groups, this procedure becomes even more important. As we know, Flickr does not explicitly take the tags into account and the number of images as a relevance criterion even less. Therefore, seven of the first eight groups in Figure 15 remain empty, while the group ranking procedure sorts the results by the number of relevant images. The relevance of the images is here is judged based on the strong commitment of the Flickr groups. The relevance of a group is not necessarily dependent on the number of matching images in a group. A group with fewer elements could well have more relevant images than one with more pictures. In this case, we can optimize the group ranking method by combining it with qRANK. Therefore, the tags of the images are evaluated within the groups by qRANK and the weight is derived based on the evaluation of the tags for the image and the group.

8.2.3 Experiment 2: Game-Based Picture Ranking with qRANK

For this experiment, we put two different versions of qRANK online for one week. The first version consisted of 250 randomly selected images for the topic "Kirche" and the second version of 100 images selected specifically for the topic of "Hund." The users should select the most relevant three terms for the image. In the first scenario a user always had to choose one of the words even if he was not sure about his choice. In the second game, the user could press a pass button to get the next picture if he could not find a suitable definition.

8.2.4 Result Experiment 2

The first variant of the qRANK was not played as often this time as originally expected, so that no term was selected more than twice. This value was too small to represent a statement about the relevance of a tag. The second variant of qRANK was played more often and due to the small amount of data provided desirable results. An evaluation of the ranked tag list of the one hundred pictures provided, showed that 56 of the pictures had their most relevant tags first. Only nine pictures did not have their most used tags in the first four positions (see **Figure 52**):

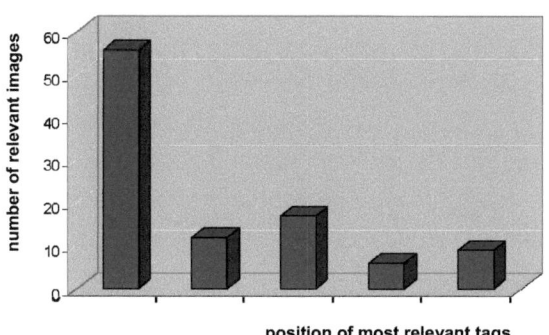

Figure 52: Positions of the most relevant tags

After a one-week game period the result was that 91% of the images played during this time, had their most relevant tags in the first four positions. These results illustrate the effect of the approach. The aim of this experiment is not necessarily to find new terms for an image, but to assess the relevance of the existing tags depending on the content of the image. In order to make a relevant statement, only images were considered, that were selected at least four times. Striking here was that users often choose terms in different languages or in plural/singular relation. So many images in the ranked tag list often appeared in different languages. Regarding the search process, this is not necessarily a disadvantage, since a user may search in different languages. For the evaluation of the concepts in qRANK, it is disadvantageous in the long run, as these are the terms preferred, and therefore reduce the probability that other terms would be selected. This problem can be limited if we can determine these relationships beforehand automatically.

8.2.5 Resume

In all, information quality enhancement is getting more and more important – especially regarding the flood of autonomous web resources without responding authorship. We presented the role of information quality in web-based information and knowledge transfer with smart interaction.

We adapted an existing assessment model to our purpose in qKAI and showed some examples of enhanced, rating-based interaction that is suitable to qualify Open Content in steps in an incentive way. Incentive for user participation and interaction is implemented in qKAI as a game-oriented, ontology-based and global rewarding model for any kind of interaction. Information quality can be utilized as a tool to derive personalization and user preferences in web-based information and knowledge systems, because it offers metrics to determine the fitness for use of autonomous, distributed resources.

The evaluation of our group ranking and game based assessing approach for Flickr images showed promising results and the content's quality increased visibly. Single tasks are reusable and combinable in different scenarios (implemented as atomic web services). It becomes possible to rate game-oriented evaluation and rating applications or rank content and opinions in a more incentive way without becoming boring.

8.3 The Impact of Rewarding Mechanisms on User Behavior

The purpose of this evaluation is to find out how rewarding mechanisms affect a user's activity behavior. In other words, if a user is being rewarded for activities, does it result in more activities compared to users that are not being rewarded. Furthermore, the importance of the different statistics Squirl offers has been evaluated, i.e. which type of statistic has been requested the most and which the least. The evaluation is based on a test application related to Flickr photo tags and titles. The main task within this test application is to rank photo tags according to their relevance. Optionally users may rate photo titles by how suitable they are for a photo and they may add new tags to a photo. This test application, which itself constitutes some kind of evaluation, is an adequate example of where the usage of rewarding mechanisms may influence user behavior in a positive way, since most participants of evaluations refer to them as a chore, therefore applying rewarding mechanisms in such scenarios may result in more and possibly better evaluation results. The setting for this evaluation will be explained in more detail in **Chapter 8.3.1** and the results it produced with respect to its impact on user behavior will be outlined in **Chapter 8.3.2**.

8.3.1 Setting

As already mentioned, the test application used for the evaluation is itself an evaluation related to Flickr photos. For this purpose, photos have been downloaded from Flickr along with their assigned titles and tags and these photos will be randomly presented to the participants. Within this test application, participants are supposed to rank tags of a photo according to their relevance and they may add new tags that they think are more relevant than the assigned ones. Additionally, users may rate photo titles on a scale of 0 to 10 depending on how well the title fits the content of a photo. In sum, this application rewards the following interactions via Squirl's REST API:

- Rank, for each tag ranked
- Tag, for each tag added
- Rate, for each photo title rated
- Explore, for each photo rewarding version or non-rewarding version explored

Figure 53: GIAR test applications (rewarding and non-rewarding version) [46]

Two versions of this test application have been implemented for this evaluation (see **Figure 53**). One version displays the number of points earned for each interaction and alerts participants if they have won an award. Furthermore, it offers access to all the statistics presented in **Chapter 7.1**, **Figure 43** and to all leaderboards available via Squirl's REST API. The other version does not display any points, statistics or leaderboards, therefore, it is a "non-rewarding" version of this test application. According to both versions, the group of participants has been partitioned into two subgroups: one uses the "rewarding" version and the other uses the "non-rewarding" version of the test application. An important requirement for this evaluation was that participants from both subgroups should not know each other, since this might have caused misunderstandings with respect to the different versions of the test application. Apart from that, the premises have been the same for both subgroups:

1. Participants do not need to rank all tags of a photo.
2. Photo title rating and the addition of new tags is optional.
3. Evaluation lasts one month.
4. There are no minimum requirements with regard to the number of photos evaluated, ranked tags or rated titles. In total, 40 people participated in this evaluation, twenty of them have been assigned accounts for the rewarding version and the others have been assigned accounts for the non-rewarding version of the test application.

8.3.2   Results and Conclusion

In total, 12,958 interactions have been executed by participants from both groups during the evaluation period. Those participants that have been using the "rewarding" version of the upper test application requested Squirl's statistics a total of 536 times. **Table 18** and the following diagrams outline the most important aspects of this result.

8 qKAI Evaluation: Proof of Concept

	group 1 (rewarded)	group 2 (not rewarded)
# of users	20	20
# of executed interactions	11682	1276
⌀ per participant	584	64
days with activity	23	10
sessions	44	20
⌀ session length	35 minutes	13 minutes
# of explore interactions	3430	536
# of tag interactions	763	143
# of rank interactions	4563	367
# of rate interactions	2926	230
ranked tags per photo	1,33	0,68
rated titles	85,31%	24,91%

Table 18: Evaluation results, rewarded versus not rewarded interaction [46]

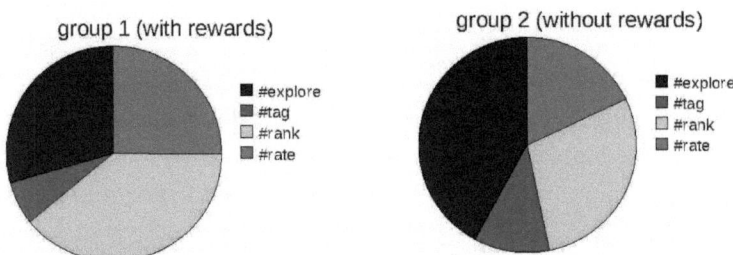

Figure 54: Interaction distribution within both evaluation groups [46]

8 qKAI Evaluation: Proof of Concept

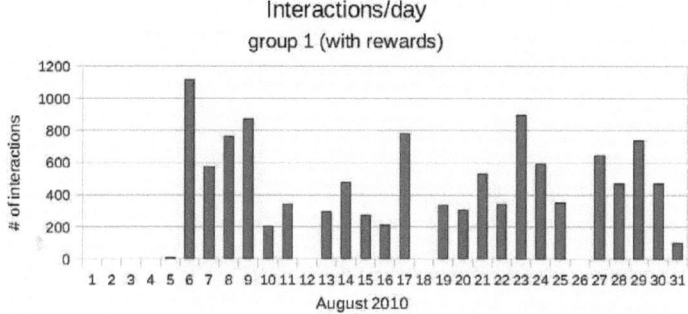

Figure 55: Interactions per day of group 1 (with rewards) during evaluation period [46]

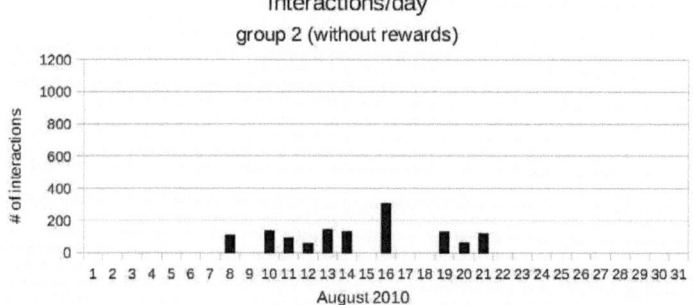

Figure 56: Interactions per day of group 2 (without rewards) during evaluation period [46]

8 qKAI Evaluation: Proof of Concept

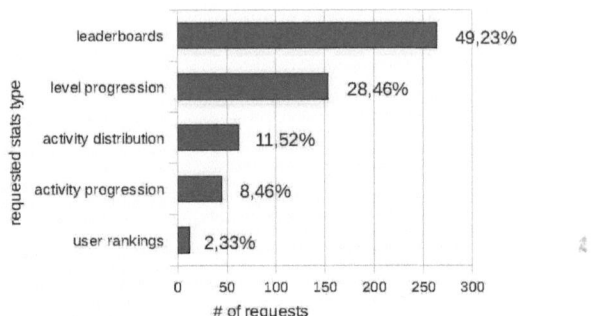

Figure 57: Requested Squirl statistics during evaluation period

8.3.3 Resume

Obviously rewarding mechanisms have an effect on user motivation considering the fact that 90% of all interactions were executed by participants from the group that used the rewarding version of the test application. **Figure 54** illustrates that almost every title of every explored picture has been rated by group 1, whereas group 2 only rated every fourth photo title. Compared to the number of explored photos within group 2, only 367 tags were ranked, i.e. only 0.68 tags per photo were ranked, whereas group 1 ranked 1.33 tags per photo. Rewarding mechanisms do not only result in more interactions, but also in more regularity as **Figures 55** and **56** illustrate. Users who are rewarded for activities tend to do more and are more consistent in the activity than users, who are not rewarded. **Figure 57** points out that it is important for users to compare themselves socially with others, as well as keep track of their progression. About 50 % of all requested Squirl statistics have been requests for leaderboards that enable social comparison and about 30% of all stats requests have been requests for level progressions, which enable users to keep track of their evolution. [46]

8.4 Summary

During this thesis three main aspects regarding the utilization of distributed resources for higher-layered applications have been evaluated to reach a "proof of concept" for the derived models explained in **Chapters 5** and **6**.

Evaluation aspect 1: Open Content can serve as a rich knowledge base for enhanced user interaction scenarios. Web services for knowledge engineering and enabling of user activity are necessary. A prototypical web service collection and an initial qKAI knowledge base are available with the qKAI mashup framework.

Evaluation aspect 2: User activity can be embedded into knowledge engineering processes to analyze and enhance content quality. The example of tag ranking in folksonomies is examined regarding grouping tasks and game-based ranking mechanisms to enhance the relevance quality of the images.

Evaluation aspect 3: Rewarding mechanisms that are adapted out of game design influence a user's motivation to activity in web applications in a positive way. With the Global Interaction Rewarding model (GIAR), qKAI offers a generic and application independent solution for a meta-rewarding system of users' activity in web applications.

9 Conclusion

The Web is omnipresent as an information and knowledge base, which is continuously increasing. The challenges involved in simplifying access to distributed web resources, to enhance their representation and interconnectivity and to create motivating user interoperation with regard to these resources are growing in importance.

This thesis analyzed current web methods and technologies to propose a new concept in utilizing distributed web resources using the example of Social Media and Linked Open Data for enhanced knowledge representation in social web applications and knowledge engineering. **Web-based game mechanics** are deployed as **interactive knowledge systems that rely on Open Content**.

The service-oriented qKAI mashup framework is a collection of software components and web services. It has been developed as a basis on which to build web applications like social networks, while using the REST architectural software style and enabling interfaces with rich user experience.

The main features of the qKAI mashup framework are:

- Support for hybrid data handling of distributed web resources as a global knowledge base, while combining a traditional relational data model with semantic resource annotation.
- Support for the global integration of gaming principles as enhanced user interaction concepts into web applications.
- Support for enhancing information quality of distributed web resources by user interaction and automatically deployed algorithms.

9 Conclusion

The derived Global Interaction Rewarding (GIAR) system uses principles and mechanics known from game design. A social interaction rewarding community, Squirl, has been implemented as an example use case of the positive conversion of gaming principles and user interaction in web-based applications.

Basic game mechanics and reward types have been successfully applied in order to reward user interactions or to give feedback on their effect on a user's progress. The thesis presented a concept that integrates an application independent model for globally rewarding user interaction tasks. The Social Interaction Taxonomy can be integrated into web applications through RESTful web services.

The taxonomy serves as a foundation for activity monitoring, interaction rewarding or analysis. It is also useful for increasing incentive and motivation to ongoing participation in social web applications are further use cases in global interaction rewarding. Basic game mechanics and reward types are presented and have been applied in order to reward user interactions or to give feedback on their effect on a user's progression. Interaction rewarding acting independently from specific web applications and especially from the interactions they offer is implemented by the Global Interaction rewarding model (GIAR).

This taxonomy classifies interactions first by its counterpart, which can be a resource or a user, and then by the way a user interacts with a resource and by the level of intensity of how a user communicates with another user. The taxonomy is ideal for classifying and rewarding activity in learning contexts because it can turn any application into a game in this way. SIT also allows tracking progress and a user's activity with regard to web-based resources.

The evaluation results showed that the applied game mechanics have a positive effect on user behavior as it resulted in many more interactions compared to participants that used the non-rewarding version of the test application.

9 Conclusion

This thesis proves that the quality of content can be enhanced by user interaction like game-based ranking procedures and machine-related algorithms shown by the example of tag ranking in folksonomies.

The derived keyword-oriented group search algorithms and the ranking game qRANK showed promising results with regard to motivating users and enhancing the content information quality. Overall, information quality can be used as a tool to derive personalization and user preferences in web-based information and knowledge systems because it offers metrics to determine the fitness for use of autonomous, distributed resources. Distributed web resources are utilized as a global knowledge base during the whole thesis. Freely available Social Media like Flickr photos and structured resources like Linked Open Data are very well suited to serving as distributed data store.

The following section summarizes the contributions of this thesis and the impact of the work. In conclusion, the direction of future research in this area is discussed.

9.1 Contributions

The main contribution of this thesis is the development of the qKAI mashup framework embedding game-oriented user interaction concepts in web-based applications with a strong focus on distributed resources in information and knowledge transfer.

The service-oriented qKAI mashup framework is implemented prototypically to fulfill necessary subtasks and involves the design of the following artifacts:

- A prototype for an **Online Communities** based upon the qKAI mashup framework (**Squirl**)
- Reusable RESTful web services with API for external web applications

9 Conclusion

- Game-oriented user interaction concepts and prototypes (proof of concept)
  - For knowledge transfer based on distributed web resources (qMATCH, qMAP)
  - To qualify and annotate distributed web resources (qRANK)
- A three-level qualifying model for distributed web resources
- A global user interaction rewarding model (GIAR)
  - With classification of web-based user interaction tasks and assigned rewards to motivate users to ongoing participation and activity in web applications
  - For integration into any web-based application and extension by further user activity tasks
- A distributed resource annotation concept following Linked Data paradigms (qKAI resource annotator)

9.2 Future Work and Outlook

The work presented in this thesis opens up several directions for future research in the related areas of knowledge engineering utilizing Social Media resources as a global knowledge base while applying gaming mechanics and information quality criteria in RESTful web applications.

This thesis concludes with the "proof of concept" and prototypical implementation of knowledge engineering services enabling semantic resource annotation, enhanced knowledge representation and global interaction rewarding.

With the qKAI mashup framework, a foundation has been laid upon which to build web-based social network applications and further mashup scenarios with a focus on Open Content out of distributed resources, information quality concerns and incentive to ongoing user attendance and interoperation.

The assessment of information quality has been shown during this work and can be extended by analyzing more metadata about resources automatically by implementing state of the art algorithms and technologies. The evaluation showed promising results for further work while at the same time integrating game mechanics and aspects of information quality into knowledge engineering based on distributed resources of Social Media and Linked Open Data.

10 Appendices

Appendix A: List of Abbreviations

AJAX	Asynchronous JavaScript and XML
API	Application Programming Interface
APP	Application
DB	Database
DBMS	Database Management System
GUI	General User Interface
(x)HTML	(extensible) Hypertext Markup Language
HTTP	Hypertext Transfer Protocol
HCI	Human Computer Interaction
IDE	Integrated Development Environment
KE	Knowledge Engineering
KM	Knowledge Management
RDF	Resource Description Framework
REST	Representational State Transfer
JSON	JavaScript Object Notation
LOD	Linked Open Data
MVC	Model View Controller
NLP	Natural Language Processing
qKAI	qualifying Knowledge Acquisition and Inquiry (PhD project title)

REST	Representational State Transfer
RIA	Rich Internet Application
SW	Semantic Web
S2W	Social Semantic Web
SOA	Service Oriented Architecture
SPARQL	SPARQL Protocol and RDF Query Language
SQL	Structured Query Language
WS	Web Service
XML	Extensible Markup Language

Appendix B: List of Figures

Figure 1: World Internet penetration rates by geographic regions in 2009 [1] 1

Figure 2: Web 3.0 tag cloud (created with Wordle [13]) 14

Figure 3: Example of a Wikipedia article about Hannover and a Freebase site about architecture in 2010. 16

Figure 4: Delicio.us [28] tags and Flickr images about the architecture in Hannover [4] 20

Figure 5: DBpedia Linked Open Data cloud [16] 23

Figure 6: Flow in games [69] 46

Figure 7: Sacred 2 skills [72] 50

Figure 8: World of Warcraft inventory [57] 50

Figure 9: Mario's 1-Up Reward [79] 51

Figure 10: Mechanics – Dynamics – Aesthetics concept (based on [84]) 55

Figure 11: Bottle Bank Arcade [52] 61

Figure 12: qKAI Open Data and knowledge cycle 73

Figure 13: qKAI and LOD cloud 76

Figure 14: Entity relation diagram for the qKAI resource annotation 77

Figure 15: (Social) Interaction Cloud 79

Figure 16: Interactions classified by its counterpart [46] 81

Figure 17: User-Resource interaction-types [46] 83

Figure 18: User-User interaction-types [46] 84

Figure 19: (Social) interaction taxonomy [46] 85

10 Appendices

Figure 20: GIAR architecture and used components (based on [46]) 86
Figure 21: GIAR levels and skills [46] 89
Figure 22: Level constants - example 1 [46] 91
Figure 23: Level constants - example 2 [46] 91
Figure 24: GIAR medals [46] 93
Figure 25: GIAR skill- and class-badges [46] 94
Figure 26: GIAR patron of the month badge [46] 94
Figure 27: Most relevant iq-criteria for the qKAI system domain: knowledge transfer and smart interaction based on autonomous resources. 101
Figure 28: Flickr standard search for the terms „Rathaus" and „Hannover". 111
Figure 29: Ranking criteria in folksonomies 114
Figure 30: Extended Flickr search for the terms „Rathaus Hannover" with precision formula 116
Figure 31: Analysis of Flickr groups "number of members" [119] 120
Figure 32: Analysis of Flickr groups "total images" [119] 121
Figure 33: Example tag distribution in a Flickr group 122
Figure 34: Power-Law curve [115] 123
Figure 35: qKAI mashup framework with system layers as conceptual design and development basis 129
Figure 36: qKAI architecture outline 131
Figure 37: Coupling of interaction related model types 138

10 Appendices

Figure 38: Interaction logging sequence 154
Figure 39: Squirl start page [46] 166
Figure 40: MySquirl — user's personal Squirl page [46] 167
Figure 41: Activity import sequence [46] 168
Figure 42: Creator of the week badge [46] 169
Figure 43: Squirl user stats [46] 170
Figure 44: qMAP frontend 173
Figure 45: Search, filter and periphery interface of qMAP 173
Figure 46: History and interaction protocol of
Open Content for statistical analysis
behind the qMAP interface. 174
Figure 47: qMATCH text image assignment game 175
Figure 48: Knowledge game result in qMATCH with own
correct answers and aggregated statistics. 176
Figure 49: qRANK: A tag rating image text assignment
game based on Flickr content 178
Figure 50: qRANK, a tag rating image text assignment
game based on Flickr content 181
Figure 51: Results of the Flickr group rating approach
ranking by the number of relevant images 188
Figure 52: Positions of the most relevant tags 189
Figure 53: GIAR test applications
(rewarding and non-rewarding version) [46] 192
Figure 54: Interaction distribution within both evaluation
groups [46] 194
Figure 55: Interactions per day of group 1
(with rewards) during evaluation period [46] 195

Figure 56: Interactions per day of group 2 (without rewards) during evaluation period [46]... 195

Figure 57: Requested Squirl statistics during evaluation period [46] 196

Appendix C: List of Tables

Table 1: Development in percent of online usage in Germany between 1997 and 2009 (occasional usage) [2] 3

Table 2: Usage of Web 2.0 offers in percent by gender and age in Germany in 2009 (occasional usage) [2] 4

Table 3: Development of occasional and frequent usage of Web 2.0 offers in percent in Germany from 2007 to 2009 5

Table 4: Iq citeria and their classification for autonomous information systems based on C. Bizer's categorization [103] 70

Table 5: Points assigned to interactions [46] 87

Table 6: Level types and aggregated interactions [46] 88

Table 7: Cron Expressions for awarding jobs [46] 96

Table 8: Exemplary Dublin Core element set for metadata [112] 104

Table 9: Interaction tasks, assigned rewarding points and improvable iq-criteria 106

Table 10: Interaction tasks, assigned rewarding points and improvable iq-criteria 107

Table 11: qKAI Data Acess Objects (DAOs) 134

Table 12: Flickr group analysis for the term "Kirche" 143

Table 13: Model types used in qKAI (especially Squirl) 145

Table 14: Resource and interface description for the qKAI resource annotator 146

Table 15: Class structure of the qKAI resource annotator services (resources)..............147

Table 16: Class structure of the qKAI resource annotator services (controller)..............148

Table 17: Class structure of the qKAI resource annotator services (model)..................149

Table 18: Evaluation results, rewarded versus not rewarded interaction [46]................194

10 Appendices

Appendix D: List of Listings

Listing 1: Java based REST resource 31
Listing 2: XML representation of a REST resource 32
Listing 3: Method to compute points needed
for a given level 90
Listing 4: Implementation of the reward
scheduling method 95
Listing 5: qKAI DAO factory 135
Listing 6: qKAI MysqlDAOFactory 135
Listing 7: Basic structure of the GIAR Config file 137
Listing 8: Configuration of the user-user
interaction class level 138
Listing 9: Configuration of the user-user
interaction class level 138
Listing 10: InteractionClass (excerpt) 139
Listing 11: InteractionType (excerpt) 139
Listing 12: GIARConfig (excerpt) 140
Listing 13: Interaction (excerpt) 140
Listing 14: InteractionLogController root resource 150
Listing 15: Interaction logging service 151
Listing 16: Interaction logging service for create activities ... 152
Listing 17: Interaction logging service for for
one-way activities 152
Listing 18: JSON response to an interaction
logging request 155
Listing 19: StatsContoller root-resource 156

Listing 20: Response to an activity leaderboard request....... 160

Listing 21: SPARQL request and qKAI question
representation: 177

Listing 22: SPARQL XML response (excerpt) and qKAI
quiz answers representation for the question...... 178

Bibliography

[1] Internet World Stats, available from World Wide Web: http://www.internetworldstats.com, last update: 2009, visited 2009-04-10.

[2] ARD/ZDF-Online study 1997–2009, available from World Wide Web (Germany): http://www.ard-zdf-onlinestudie.de/?id=onlinenutzung, last update: 2009, visited 2009-05-15.

[3] Berners-Lee, T. Web 2.0 and Semantic Web, W3C, available from World Wide Web: http://www.w3.org/2006/Talks/1108-swui-tbl/#(1), last update: 2010, visited 2009-04-10.

[4] Wikipedia: Wikipedia (about itself), available from World Wide Web: http:// en.wikipedia.org, http://en.wikipedia.org/wiki/Wikipedia, last update: 2010, visited: 2010-08-05.

[5] YouTube: a video sharing community, available from World Wide Web: http://www.youtube.com, last update: 2010, visited 2010-05-27.

[6] Flickr: share your photos — watch the world, available from World Wide Web: http://www.flickr.com/, last update: 2010, visited 2010-05-16.

[7] Panoramio: a photo sharing community, available from World Wide Web: http://www.panoramio.com, last update: 2009, visited 2009-05-22.

[8] Cultural Council (Kulturrat) Germany, available from World Wide Web: http://www.kulturrat.de/detail.php?detail=1285, last update: 2010, visited: 2010-05-10.

[9] Bizer, C., Heath, T. and Berners-Lee, T. "Linked Data: Principles and State of the Art." In Proc. 17th International World Wide Web Conference, WWW2008, China, 2008.

[10] Wikipedia: World Wide Web, available from World Wide Web: http://en.wikipedia.org/wiki/World_Wide_Web, last update: 2010, visited 2009-05-27.

[11] Wikipedia: Web 2.0, available from World Wide Web: http://en.wikipedia.org/wiki/Web_2.0, last update: 2009, visited 2009-05-20.

[12] Wikipedia: Social Semantic Web, available from World Wide Web: http://en.wikipedia.org/wiki/Social_Semantic_Web, last update: 2010, visited 2010-09-20.

[13] Wordle: a toy for generating word clouds, available from World Wide Web: http://www.wordle.net, last update: 2009, visited 2009-05-18.

[14] Twine: an online, social web service for information storage, authoring and discovery, available from World Wide Web: http://www.twine.com/, last update: 2008, visited 2008-05-27.

[15] Freebase: a large collaborative knowledge base, available from World Wide Web: http://www.freebase.com, last update: 2009, visited 2009-05-25.

[16] DBpedia: a project aiming to extract structured information from the information created as part of the Wikipedia project, available from World Wide Web: http://dbpedia.org/About, last update: 2009, visited 2009-05-20.

[17] Becker, C. and Bizer, C. "DBpedia Mobile: A Location Enabled Linked Data Browser." In Proc. 17th International World Wide Web Conference WWW2008, China, 2008.

[18] Domenig, M. Rich Internet Applications und AJAX, Entwickler-Magazin, available from World Wide Web: http://www.canoo.com/news/entwickler.pdf, 2006, last update: 2009, visited 2009-05-15.

[19] Twitter: a microblogging service, available from World Wide Web: http://www.twitter.com, last update: 2010, visited: 2010-10-15.

[20] Rotz, B.v.: Erfolgreiche Online Communities I, available from World Wide Web: http://www.contentmanager.de/magazin/artikel_1766_online_communities.html, last update: 2010, visited 2010-08-15.

[21] Faviki: tags that make sense, available from World Wide Web: http://www.faviki.com/pages/welcome/, last update: 2009, visited 2009-05-25.

[22] Facebook: a social network service and website, available from World Wide Web: http://www.facebook.com, last update: 2010, visited: 2010-08-22.

[23] Last.fm: a music website, available from World Wide Web: http://www.last.fm/, last update: 2010, visited: 2010-08-22.

[24] Foursquare: a location-based social networking website, available from World Wide Web: http://www.foursquare.com, last update: 2010, visited: 2010-05-20.

[25] LinkedIn: a business-oriented social networking site, available from World Wide Web: http://www.likedin.com, last update: 2010, visited: 2010-05-20.

[26] Dailymile: track your workouts, a social networking website, available from World Wide Web: http://www.dailymile.com/, last update: 2010, visited 2010-10-27.

[27] Wikipedia: Soziales Netzwerk, available from World Wide Web: http://de.wikipedia.org/wiki/Soziales_Netzwerk_(Internet), last update: 2010, visited: 2010-10-11.

[28] Del.icio.us: a social bookmarking service, available from World Wide Web: http://delicio.us, last update: 2010, visited: 2010-11-10.

[29] Open Knowledge Foundation, The Open Knowledge Definition, available from World Wide Web: http://opendefinition.org/, last update: 2009, visited 2009-05-25.

[30] Resource Description Framework (RDF), available from World Wide Web: http://www.w3.org/RDF/, W3C, last update: 2008, visited 2010-05-25.

[31] SPARQL Protocol and RDF Query Language, available from World Wide Web: http://www.w3.org/TR/rdf-sparql-query/, W3C, last update: 2010, visited 2010-05-25.

[32] Fensel, J. H. D., Lieberman, H. and Wahlster, W. Spinning the Semantic Web: Bringing the World Wide Web to Its Full Potential. The Mit Press, Massachusetts, 2005.

[33] JSON (JavaScript object notation), available from World Wide Web: http://www.json.org/, last update: 2010, visited 2010-10-05.

[34] Bizer, C; Cyganiak, R. D2R server: Publishing Relational Databases on the Semantic Web, available from World Wide Web: http://www4.wiwiss.fu-berlin.de/bizer/d2r-server/, last update: 2010, visited 2009-05-27.

[35] Aperture, available from World Wide Web: http://aperture.sourceforge.net/, Aduna, DFKI, last update: 2010, visited 2009-05-27.

[36] Openlink Virtuoso, available from World Wide Web: http://virtuoso.openlinksw.com/, last update: 2010, visited 2009-05-27.

[37] OpenNLP, available from World Wide Web: http://opennlp.sourceforge.net/, last update: 2009, visited 2009-05-27.

[38] Wikipedia: Linked Open Data (LOD), available from World Wide Web: http://en.wikipedia.org/wiki/Semantic_Web#Linking_Open_Data, last update: 2010, visited 2009-05-27.

[39] Halpin, H., Presutti, V. "An Ontology of Resources for Linked Data." In Proc. LDOW 2009, April 20–24, Madrid, Spain, 2009, ACM 978-1-60558-487-4/09/04.

[40] Fielding, R. Architectural Styles and the Design of Network-based Software Architectures, Dissertation. Irvine, 2000.

[41] Wikipedia: REST, Representational State Transfer, available from World Wide Web: http://en.wikipedia.org/wiki/Representational_State_Transfer, last update: 2010, visited 2009-05-27.

[42] Wikipedia: Web services, available from World Wide Web: http://en.wikipedia.org/wiki/Web_service, last update: 2010, visited 2009-05-27.

[43] Jax-RS: Java API for restful Web services, available from World Wide Web: http://jcp.org/en/jsr/detail?id=311, last update: 2010, visited 2010-08-23.

[44] Java EE at a glance. Available from World Wide Web: http://java.sun.com/javaee/, last update: 2010, visited 2010-08-23.

[45] Jersey, available from World Wide Web: https://jersey.dev.java.net/, last update: 2010, visited 2010-05-27.

[46] Ullmann, N. Design and implementation of a global rewarding model based on user interaction tasks, master thesis, qKAI project. Leibniz Universität Hannover, System and Computer Architecture (SRA), 2010.

[47] Wikipedia: AJAX, Asynchronous JavaScript, available from World Wide Web: http://en.wikipedia.org/wiki/Ajax_programming, last update: 2010, visited 2009-05-27.

[48] Adobe Flash/Flex, available from World Wide Web: http://www.adobe.com/products/flex/, visited 2009-07-05,

[49] Nov, O. What motivates Wikipedians, Communications of the ACM, 50(11):60–64, 2007.

[50] Wikipedia: Interaction design, available from World Wide Web: http://en.wikipedia.org/wiki/Interaction_design#Interaction_design_domains, last update: 2010, visited: 2010-10-10.

[51] Prensky, M. Digital Game-Based Learning, Chapter 5, pages 5, 6. McGraw-Hill, New York, 2001.

[52] Volkswagen initiative, The Fun Theory, http://www.thefuntheory.com, last update: 2009, visited: 2010-10-10.

[53] Kim, A.J. Putting the fun in functional - applying game mechanics to Social Media, 2009, available from World Wide Web: http://www.slideshare.net/amyjokim/fun-in-functional-2009-presentation, last update: 2009, visited: 2010-10-10.

[54] Ahn, L. Games with a Purpose. Carnegie Mellon University, Invisible Computing, Juli 2006.

[55] Amazon, available from World Wide Web: http://www.amazon.com, last update: 2010, visited: 2010-05-20.

[56] Salen, K., Zimmerman, E. Rules of Play: Game Design Fundamentals. MIT Press, 2003, ISBN 978-0262240451.

[57] Golem Special: World of Warcraft, available from World Wide Web: http://www.golem.de/specials/wow/, last update: 2010, visited: 2010-10-10.

[58] Crumlish, C. Learn from Games, http://www.designingsocialinterfaces.com/patterns/Learn_from_Games, last update: 2010, visited: 2010-10-10.

[59] Berne, E. Games People Play, http://www.ericberne.com/Games_People_Play.htm, last update: 2010, visited 2009-05-25.

[60] Wikipedia: Pong, available from World Wide Web: http://en.wikipedia.org/wiki/Pong, last update: 2010, visited: 2010-09-12.

[61] Wikipedia: Game development, available from World Wide Web: http://en.wikipedia.org/wiki/Game_development, last update: 2010, visited: 2010-09-12.

[62] Wikipedia: Game design, available from World Wide Web: http://en.wikipedia.org/wiki/Game_design, last update: 2010, visited: 2010-09-12.

[63] Wikipedia: Homo ludens, 2010, available from World Wide Web: http://de.wikipedia.org/wiki/Homo_ludens, last update: 2010, visited: 2010-09-12.

[64] Huizinga, J. Homo Ludens: A Study of the Play-Element in Culture. Beacon Press, June 1971.

[65] Prensky, M. Digital Game-Based Learning, Chapter 5, pages 12,13,14,15. McGraw-Hill, New York, 2001.

[66] Wikipedia. Massively multiplayer online role-playing game, 2010, available from World Wide Web: http://en.wikipedia.org/wiki/Massively_multiplayer_online_role-playing_game, last update: 2010, visited: 2010-09-12.

[67] Devil may cry, available from World Wide Web: http://www.devilmaycry.com/home.html, last update: 2010, visited: 2010-09-12.

[68] Sim City, available from World Wide Web: http://simcity.ea.com, last update: 2009, visited: 2010-09-12.

[69] Csikszentmihalyi, M., Abuhamdeh, S. and Nakamura, J. "Flow." In: Handbook of Competence and Motivation, editors Elliot and Dweck, pages 598–698, The Guilford Press, 2005.

[70] Wikipedia: Massively multiplayer online role-playing game, available from World Wide Web: http://en.wikipedia.org/wiki/Tetris, last update: 2010, visited: 2010-09-12.

[71] Prensky, M. Digital Game-Based Learning, Chapter 5, page 15. McGraw-Hill, New York, 2001.

[72] Ascaron, Sacred 2 - fallen angel, available from World Wide Web: http://www.sacred2.com, last update: 2009, last update: 2010, visited: 2010-09-12.

[73] Porter, J. Game mechanics for interaction design: An interview with Amy Jo Kim, available from World Wide Web: http://bokardo.com/archives/game-mechanics-for-interaction-design-an-interview-with-amy-jo-kim/, last update: 2009, visited: 2010-09-12.

[74] Kim, A.J. Putting the fun in functional - applying game mechanics to functional software, available from World Wide

Web: http://www.slideshare.net/amyjokim/putting-the-fun-in-functional, last update: 2007, visited: 2009-09-12.

[75] Payback, available from World Wide Web: http://www.payback.de/, last update: 2010, visited: 2010-09-17.

[76] Farmville, available from World Wide Web: http://www.facebook.com/FarmVille, last update: 2010, visited: 2010-09-12.

[77] Casual Game Design, the reward series, part 1: The basics of reward, 2006, available from World Wide Web: http://www.casualgamedesign.com/?p=42, last update: 2006, visited: 2010-09-12.

[78] Civilization, available from World Wide Web: http://www.civilization.com/, last update: 2010, visited: 2010-09-12.

[79] Super Mario Bros, Wii, available from World Wide Web: http://www. mariobroswii.com/, last update: 2009, visited: 2010-09-12.

[80] Prensky, M. Digital Game-Based Learning, in Chapter 5, pages 20, 21. McGraw-Hill, New York, 2001.

[81] Bartle, R. Heart, clubs, diamonds, spades: Players who suit muds, 1996. Available from World Wide Web: http://www.mud.co.uk/richard/hcds.html, last update: 1996, visited: 2010-09-12.

[82] Spaulding, K. Video game aesthetics: Characteristics of electronic games, 2009, available from World Wide Web: http://knol.google.com/k/video-game-aesthetics, last update: 2009, visited: 2010-09-12.

[83] Nintendo. Wii console, available from World Wide Web: http://www.nintendo.com/wii/console, last update: 2010, visited: 2010-10-09.

[84] LeBlanc, M., Hunicke, R. and Zubek, R. Mda: A formal approach to game design and game research, Technical Report, Northwestern University – Electrical Engineering & Computer Science, Chicago, 2004.

[85] Ahn, L., Ginosar, S., Kedia, M., Liu, R. and Blum, M. "Improving Accessibility of the Web with a Computer Game." In Proc. International conference for human-computer interaction, CHI 2006, Canada.

[86] Mechanical Turk, available from World Wide Web: https://www.mturk.com/mturk/welcome, last update: 2010, visited: 2010-02-08.

[87] GuessTheGoogle, available from World Wide Web: http://grant.robinson.name/projects/guess-the-google/, last update: 2009, visited 2009-05-27.

[88] Scoyo, www.scoyo.de, last update: 2010, visited: 2010-05-14.

[89] Open definition, available from World Wide Web: http://www.opendefinition.org/, last update: 2010, visited: 2010-05-14.

[90] Playfish, http://www.playfish.com, last update: 2010, visited: 2010-05-14.

[91] Megazebra, available from World Wide Web: http://www.megazebra.com, last update: 2010, visited: 2010-05-14.

[92] Zynga, available from World Wide Web: www.zynga.com, last update: 2010, visited: 2010-05-14.

[93] MySpace, available from World Wide Web: http://www.myspace.com, last update: 2010, visited: 2010-05-14.

[94] Braingame, available from World Wide Web: http://www.braingame.de, last update: 2010, visited: 2010-05-14.

[95] IMS/QTI, available from World Wide Web: http://www.imsglobal.org/question/, IMS Global Learning Consortium, Inc., last update: 2008, visited 2009-05-25.

[96] Mungai, D., Jones, D., Wong, L. "Games to Teach By." In Proc. 18th Annual Conference on Distance Teaching and Learning, 2005.

[97] Britannica: Online Encyclopedia, http://www.britannica.com/, last update: 2010, visited: 2010-05-20.

[98] Wikipedia: Gamification, available from World Wide Web: http://en.wikipedia.org/wiki/Gamification, last update: 2011, visited: 2011-02-02.

[99] Heise online News, available from World Wide Web: http://www.heise.de/newsticker/meldung/Nature-Wikipedia-nahe-an-Encyclopaedia-Britannica-158194.html, last update: 2008, visited: 2009-07-20.

[100] Naumann, F. "Quality-Driven Query Answering for Integrated Information Systems." Lecture Notes in Computer Science Vol. 2261, Springer, 2002.

[101] Kruse, P., Warnke, T., Dittler, A., Gebel, T. Wertewelt Medien, available from World Wide Web: http://www.nextpractice.de/fileadmin/studien/medienstudie2007/Medienstudie_Nov2007.pdf, last update: 2007, visited: 2008-04-10.

[102] Juran, J. The Quality Control Handbook. McGraw-Hill, New York, 3rd edition, 1974.

[103] Bizer, C. Quality-Driven Information Filtering in the Context of Web-Based Information Systems, Dissertation, 2007.

[104] Mui, L. Computational Models of Trust and Reputation: Agents, Evolutionary Games and Social Networks, Dissertation, 2003.

[105] Parker, M., Moleshe, V., De La Harpe, R., Wills, G. An evaluation of Information quality frameworks for the World Wide Web, Cape Peninsula University of Technology, University of Southampton, available from World Wide Web: http://de.scientificcommons.org/14463068, last update: 2006, visited: 2008-04-10.

[106] Wand, Y., Wang. R. "Anchoring Data Quality Dimensions in Ontological Foundations," Communications of the ACM, 39(11):86–95, 1996.

[107] Heath, T. and Motta, E. Revyu.com: a Reviewing and Rating Site for the Web of Data, in Proc. ISWC 2007, International Semantic Web Conference, in Lecture Notes in Computer Science 4825 Springer 2007, pp. 895–902.

[108] Abel, F., Frank, M., Henze, N., Krause, D. and Siehndel, P. Groupme! - combining ideas of wikis, social bookmarking, and blogging, editors Adar, Hurst, Finin, Glance, Nicolov, and Tseng, ICWSM, the AAAI Press, 2008.

[109] Quartz — enterprise job scheduler, available from World Wide Web: http://www.quartz-scheduler.org/, last update: 2010, visited: 2010-07-10.

[110] Seaman. Exp chart, 2007, available from World Wide Web: http://forum.vc.igg.com/viewthread.php?tid=11992, last update: 2009, visited: 2010-07-10.

[111] Jøsang, A., Ismail, R. and Boyd, C. A Survey of Trust and Reputation Systems for Online Service Provision, 2006.

[112] ISO 15836:2003, Information and Documentation – The Dublin Core Metadata Element Set. International Organization for Standardization, 2003.

[113] San Pedro, J., Siersdorfer, S. "Ranking and classifying attractiveness of photos in folksonomies." In Proc. 18th international conference on World wide Web, WWW '09, pages 771–780, New York, NY, USA, 2009. ACM.

[114] Li, X., Snoek C. and Worring, M. "Learning tag relevance by neighbor voting for social image retrieval." In Proc. 1st ACM international conference on Multimedia information retrieval, MIR '08, pages 180–187, New York, NY, USA, 2008. ACM.

[115] Stock, W., Peters, I. "Folksonomies in Wissensrepräsentation und Information Retrieval." In Information – Wissenschaft und Praxis 59 (2008) 2, pages 77–90, 2008.

[116] Garg, N., Weber, I. "Personalized tag suggestion for flickr." In WWW '08: In Proc. 17th international conference on World Wide Web, pages 1063–1064, New York, NY, USA, 2008. ACM.

[117] Wu, L., Yang, L., Yu, N. and Hua, X. "Learning to tag." In Proc. 18th International World Wide Web Conference, pages 361–371, April 2009.

[118] Vogel, A., Anderson, A., Raghunathan, K. Tagez: Flickr tag recommendation. 2008.

[119] Negoescu, R., Gatica-Perez, D. "Analyzing flickr groups." In Proc. CIVR '08, international conference on Content-based image and video retrieval, pages 417–426, New York, NY, USA, 2008. ACM.

[120] Abel, F., Henze, N., Krause, D. and Kriesell, M. On the effect of group structures on ranking strategies in folksonomies, Weaving Services and People on the World Wide Web, pages 275–300, 2008.

[121] Wang, G., Hoiem, D. "Learning Image Similarity from Flickr Groups Using Stochastic Intersection Kernel Machines." In Proc. ICCV 2009.

[122] Abel, F., Frank, M., Henze, N., Krause, D., Plappert, D. and Siehnde, P. Groupme! — Where Semantic Web meets Web 2.0, in Proc. ISWC/ASWC 2007, LNCS 4825, pages 871–878, 2008.

[123] Abel, F., Henze, N. and Krause, D. "Groupme!" In Proc. WWW, pages 1147–1148, 2008.

[124] Sarioglu, O. Design and implementation of a map-based frontend with geocoded knowledge units, master thesis, qKAI project, Leibniz Universität Hannover, System- and Computer Architecture, 2009.

[125] Schroth, C.; Janner, T. Web 2.0 and SOA: Converging Concepts Enabling the Internet of Services, IT Professional, Volume 9, Issue 3, 2007, pp 36– 41.

[126] Wiederhold, G. "Mediators in the Architecture of Future Information Systems." IEEE Computer, in Journal, 25(3), 38– 49, 1992.

[127] Naumann, F. Mediator/Wrapper-Architektur & Peer-Data-Management, lecture in information integration, Berlin, Humboldt Universität, last update: 2004.

[128] DWR: Direct Web Remoting, available from World Wide Web: http://directwebremoting.org/dwr/index.html, last update: 2010, visited: 2010-07-10.

[129] Springsource, available from World Wide Web: http://www.springsource. org/, last update: 2010, visited: 2010-05-14.

[130] Apache tomcat, available from World Wide Web: http://tomcat.apache.org/, last update: 2010, visited: 2010-05-14.

[131] Java architecture for xml binding, 2010, available from World Wide Web: https://jaxb.dev.java.net, last update: 2010, visited: 2010-07-10.

[132] MySQL, available from World Wide Web: http://www.mysql.com, last update: 2010, visited: 2010-05-14.

[133] Wikipedia. Data access object, 2010, available from World Wide Web: http://en.wikipedia.org/wiki/Data_access_object, last update: 2010, visited: 2010-07-10.

[134] Jovancevic, A. Analysis and extension of interaction with Open Content in the Social Semantic Web, master thesis, qKAI project, Leibniz Universität Hannover, System and Computer Architecture, 2009.

[135] Hotho, A., Jäschke, R., Schmitz, C. and Stumme, G. "Folkrank: A ranking algorithm for folksonomies." In: Proc. FGIR 2006, 2006.

[136] Abel, F., Henze, N. and Krause, D. "Context-aware ranking algorithms in folksonomies." In WEBIST, pages 167–174, 2009.

[137] Sigurbjörnsson, B., van Zwol, R. "Flickr tag recommendation based on collective knowledge." In: Proc. WWW08, 17th international conference on World Wide Web, pages 327–336, New York, NY, USA, 2008, ACM.

[138] Marlow, C., Naaman, M., Boyd, D. and Davis, M. "HT06, tagging paper, taxonomy, Flickr, academic article, to read." In: Proc. HYPERTEXT '06, seventeenth conference on Hypertext and hypermedia, pages 31–40, New York, NY, USA, 2006. ACM.

[139] Wikipedia: Javabean, 2010, available from World Wide Web: http://en.wikipedia.org/wiki/JavaBean, last update: 2010, visited: 2010-07-10.

[140] Apple iPhone, available from World Wide Web: http://www.apple.com/iphone/, last update: 2010, visited: 2010-07-10.

[141] Wikipedia: Mashup (Web application hybrid), available from World Wide Web: http://en.wikipedia.org/wiki/Mashup_(web_application_hybrid), last update: 2010, visited: 2010-05-14.

[142] DBpedia dataset classification, available from World Wide Web: http://wiki.dbpedia.org/Datasets, last update: 2010, visited: 2010-05-14.

i want morebooks!

Buy your books fast and straightforward online - at one of world's fastest growing online book stores! Environmentally sound due to Print-on-Demand technologies.

Buy your books online at
www.get-morebooks.com

Kaufen Sie Ihre Bücher schnell und unkompliziert online – auf einer der am schnellsten wachsenden Buchhandelsplattformen weltweit! Dank Print-On-Demand umwelt- und ressourcenschonend produziert.

Bücher schneller online kaufen
www.morebooks.de

VDM Verlagsservicegesellschaft mbH
Heinrich-Böcking-Str. 6-8
D - 66121 Saarbrücken

Telefon: +49 681 3720 174
Telefax: +49 681 3720 1749

info@vdm-vsg.de
www.vdm-vsg.de

Printed by Books on Demand GmbH, Norderstedt / Germany